How to Fix Your Credit Score

Repair Your Credit and Improve Your Score Quickly. Repair Your Credit Report, Remove Your Bad Credit and Improve Your Financial Situation.

By *Reginald J. Kunz*

© Copyright 2019 - Reginald J. Kunz - All rights reserved.

The content contained within this book may not be reproduced, duplicated or transmitted without direct written permission from the author or the publisher.

Under no circumstances will any blame or legal responsibility be held against the publisher, or author, for any damages, reparation, or monetary loss due to the information contained within this book. Either directly or indirectly.

Legal Notice:

This book is copyright protected. This book is only for personal use. You cannot amend, distribute, sell, use, quote or paraphrase any part, or the content within this book, without the consent of the author or publisher.

Disclaimer Notice:

Please note the information contained within this document is for educational and entertainment purposes only. All effort has been executed to present accurate, up to date, and reliable, complete information. No warranties of any kind are declared or implied. Readers acknowledge that the author is not engaging in the rendering of legal, financial, medical or professional advice. The content within this book has been derived from various sources. Please consult a licensed professional before attempting any techniques outlined in this book.

By reading this document, the reader agrees that under no circumstances is the author responsible for any losses, direct or indirect, which are incurred as a result of the use of information contained within this document, including, but not limited to, — errors, omissions, or inaccuracies.

Table of Contents

Chapter 1: Understanding Credit Scoring ___1
Chapter 2: What's a Good Credit Score? ___12
Understanding FICO Credit Score ___12
How to Obtain a Good Credit Score: ___17
Finding out your Rico scores ___26
Tips for raising your FICO scores ___27
How Credit Scoring Came into Being ___28
The Difference Between Credit Scores & Credit Reports. ___30
Your Credit Report ___31
Getting Your Credit Report ___32
How to Fix your Credit Score Report Errors ___35
Know the difference between a "soft inquiry" and a "hard inquiry." ___44

Chapter 3: Credit Scoring Myth ___45
Chapter 4: Credit Bureau ___60
Origin and History of Credit Bureau ___61
What Credit Bureaus Do? ___63
Three Major Credit Bureau ___65

Chapter 5: Section 609 ___68
WHY & HOW The Section 609 Credit Dispute DIY Letter Works. ___77
The Dispute Process ___85
Tips for Your Dispute Letter ___89

Chapter 6: Fixing Your Credit Score Fast ___95
Boosting Your Score in 30 to 60 Days ___101
What Typically Doesn't Work ___106

Chapter 7: Managing Debt ___109
What's the Best Approach to Deal with Huge Credit Card Debt? ___111

Chapter 8: Loans and Your Credit Score ___126

Chapter 1: Understanding Credit Scoring

Your credit score is regarded as one of the most crucial factors in your financial life. It decides whether you will be affirmed for a loan or line of credit. A credit score is a numerically determined number created by the Fair Isaac Corporation (FICO) that lenders use to rate potential clients in deciding the probability that a client will take care of their bills on schedule. A credit score or credit rating is dictated by utilizing five fundamental criteria as characterized by MyFico.com: your installment history which accounts for 35% of your credit score, the sums owed which accounts for 30% of your credit score, the length of your credit history which accounts for 15% of your credit score, new credit which accounts for 10% of your credit score, and the kinds of credit utilized which accounts for 10% of your credit score.

Installment history shows the history of how you took care of your tabs either on schedule or late yet sadly doesn't appear if your bills were paid before the due date. Sums owed shows the aggregate sum of credit you have accessible. If that your parity is close to as far as possible, this may bring down your credit score. The length of history shows to what extent you have had credit. If that your credit history is 2 years or less could bring down your credit score. New credit demonstrates how frequently you have applied for new credit. In the event that you open two numerous new accounts in a brief timeframe, this may bring down your credit score. The sorts of credit utilized demonstrate the kinds of accounts you have, for example, rotating or installment accounts. Rotating accounts are typically credit cards, and installment accounts are generally contracts, automobile loans, and so on.

The FICO credit score model extents from 300-850, with 850 being a phenomenal score and 300 being the most exceedingly awful score. The lower the financing cost you will get for a loan or credit extension as your credit score goes higher. Having a good credit score can spare you a huge number of dollars in enthusiasm over the life of the loan or credit extension. A good credit score is generally in the scope of 660-749 yet may vary from lender to lender.

The three significant credit agencies Experian, Equifax, and TransUnion, utilize the FICO credit score model. Equifax utilizes the Beacon credit score, Experian utilizes the Fair Isaac or Plus score, and TransUnion utilizes the Empirica score. Each credit agency buys in to the Fair Isaac's FICO model of scoring and afterward incorporates their own adaptation of a customer's FICO score. The Equifax Beacon score ranges from 340-820. The TransUnion Empirica score ranges from 150-934. The Fair Isaac or Plus score ranges from 330-830.

While applying for credit or a loan, if each of the three credit scores are pulled, the center score is generally the score utilized with the application, however as indicated by the Fair Isaac

Corporation 75% of home loan applications utilize the Fair Isaac or Plus score.

Your credit score shifts from every authority on the grounds that every organization gathers their own information from different sources and may gather various information for a similar record. Your score can vary somewhere in the range of 5-40 points between the three credit authorities. Your credit score changes because of updates to your credit file, which changes dependent on account movement, for example, balance changes or increases to your credit file (for example, new accounts or erasure of more established negative accounts more than 7 or 10 years of age). Subsequently, you may see a distinction in your score starting with one month then onto the next.

The following criteria are not included in calculating your credit score:

1. If rent or you own a home
2. Income
3. Length of time at your current job
4. Length of time at your current address
5. Whether you've been denied credit

However, the above may be considered in approval for a loan in addition to using your credit score.

If you possess a low credit score here are 5 things you can do to boost your credit score:

1. Stop utilizing your credit cards and pay with cash.

2. Pay more than the monthly minimum. If you can't, it's time to cut spending.

3. Develop a plan to reduce your total debt.

4. Reduce your interest rates, but be careful of the fine print--a credit card with 0% interest could cost you thousands in interest depending on how the credit card is structured.

5. Get a part-time job in addition to your full time job or find ways to reduce expenses and use the extra money to pay down debt.

The significant hindrance of credit scoring is that it depends on information in your credit report, which may contain blunders. It is evaluated that 75% of credit reports contain at any rate one mistake. That is the reason it is critical to the point that you check your credit report in any event once per year to guarantee that all information is exact and modern.

In the event that you plan on buying an enormous thing, for example, a vehicle, house, or speculation property, it is ideal to destroy your credit yourself to check whether any negative things show up so you can fix those issues before applying for a loan.

The most ideal approach to comprehend your credit score is to do research and peruse the information that is given when you request your credit report.

Credit scoring is a convoluted procedure, and every one of the 3 significant credit stores have their very personal credit scoring models set up to decide a borrower's credit score. The 3 primary credit archives are Experian, Equifax, and TransUnion. Equifax possesses credit scores that range from a most reduced conceivable score of 300 and a most elevated conceivable score of 850. Experian has a range of340-820 and TransUnion 150-934. Much the same as PCs have redesigned working frameworks throughout the years, for example, Windows 98, Windows 2000, and Windows XP, the credit scoring framework variants update intermittently too. Not all lenders utilize a similar variant or the most refreshed adaptation while acquiring a credit report and credit score for a borrower. Along these lines, this is one motivation behind why you may have varying credit scores between one lender and another. There are five significant segments or factors that help to decide your credit score. Around 35% of your credit score is gotten from your payment history, 30 percent from the amount you owe contrasted with the amount you have accessible, 15 percent originates from 10 percent from new credit, length of credit history, and late request, and the last 10 percent originates from different things, for example, the blend of credit you at present have. Next, we will talk about every one of the five parts in further detail and clarify the fundamental principals with respect to how credit scoring functions. This information is to be utilized uniquely to help instruct and as a manual for help with the essential thoughts engaged with credit scoring.

Payment History (35%)

Your payment history is the most essential factor of credit scoring. Liquidations, assortment accounts, slow pays, and late payments, dispossessions, decisions, and liens can negatively affect your credit score. Notwithstanding, a set up history of on-time payments and a spotless credit history will decidedly affect your credit scores and help to expand them after some time. The more established any negative credit history or unfriendly credit factors are, the less they will negatively affect your credit score. In this manner, later late payments or other critical credit will negatively affect your credit a lot more noteworthy than matured awful credit.

Revolving Credit Balances to Maximum Limits (30%)

The second greatest factor in credit scoring originates from how you use your revolving credit. The credit scoring models are going to look vigorously upon what amount revolving credit you have accessible contrasted with the amount you have utilized. For credit scoring purposes, having all revolving credit or credit card accounts maximized to their limits is certifiably not a good thing, nor is it going to help better your credit scores. You would prefer not to satisfy the entirety of your revolving credit accounts since that won't show the credit authorities how well you deal with your credit. Your optimal credit proportions ought to be about 20-40 percent utilization. This means in the event that you have a credit card with a $1000 limit; you would prefer not to max. out the credit card balance, yet you would need to keep up a balance somewhere in the range of 200 and 400 dollars. If that you do understand that you have acquired more than 50% of your accessible credit limit on your card or your balance is drawing near to your limit, you ought to either attempt to pay your balance down to the 40% check or call your credit card organization and check whether they can raise your limit. The greatest mix-up you can make is to give your balance a chance to surpass your most extreme credit limit.

Length of Credit History (15%)

The more extended and progressively settled your credit history is, the better and increasingly positive of an impact it can make. Somebody who takes care of their tabs on schedule for a multi year timeframe is a greatly improved hazard than somebody who just has a 1 year history of taking care of their tabs on schedule, regardless of whether the two of them convey a similar credit score. At the point when you pay off credit card accounts, don't close them, keep them open and use them occasionally so as to keep on building a built up length of credit. Shutting your accounts can really have to a greater extent a negative affect on your credit score because of limiting the length of time that specific record was open for. The more you have built up credit accounts, the better it is for you. It is conceivable to even now have a good credit score with a short credit history; anyway, lenders may not support you for ideal financing choices because of the absence of history still.

New Credit and Inquiries (10%)

The extent of new credit you have opened will have to some degree a minor impact on your credit scores. In the event that you have various inquiries coming about because of applying for a ton of new credit and include numerous new exchange lines your credit report, this can damagingly affect your credit score. To begin with, it might negatively affect your scores since you have a great deal of new, un-built up accounts. Second, it can negatively impact your score since you have a great deal of inquiries with different lenders for different types of financing over a brief timeframe. Credit inquiries can affect your credit score, not a ton, however enough to bring down your score. This isn't to say don't shop around or don't have more than one firm pull your credit when hoping to purchase a vehicle or a home. You certainly should use due ingenuity and shop between a few lenders to ensure you are getting a good arrangement. At the point when you are contrasting statements, in any case, you should attempt to do the entirety of your shopping inside a multi day max. timeframe. All inquiries that are made while applying for an auto loan or a mortgage loan are treated as just a single inquiry when they are done inside a multi day timeframe. Along these lines If that you are ever advised to not have any other person pull your credit or else your scores will be reduced, this has a meagre truth to it. There is just one kind of credit inquiry that checks toward your credit score. That one sort of inquiry is the point at which you are making an application for credit, for example, a home loan, auto loan, credit card, and so on... At the point when you pull your very own credit, a creditor you as of now have a record with pulls your credit, or potentially a planned manager pulls your credit, these don't have any impact on your scores. Understanding this can assist you with ensuring that you don't succumb to the entirety of the urban fantasies in regards to credit inquiries.

Types and Mixture of Credit (10%)

Having a mixture of the different types of credit will smallly affect your credit scores. For a person who has a good mixture of credit, for example, a home loan, auto loan, 2-4 credit cards, and possibly a personal loan, this could be regarded a good mixture of credit versus an alternate person who has 15 credit cards and no other credit. The perfect number of credit cards to keep up is 2-4. Additionally, different types of liabilities are imperative to have, for example, installment loans and a mortgage loan.

"Knowledge is power," and the most important advance to applying for a loan is to comprehend your credit report, your credit scores and how credit scoring functions. It is highly recommended that each person checks their credit report in any event once every year to help shield themselves from off base information and from fraud. Another law was as of late passed that allows a borrower to approach their credit report one time every year for no charge to permit them the chance to audit their credit history and check the exactness of all things recorded. You are allowed to obtain a credit report from every one of the three credit repositories, TransUnion, Equifax, and Experian. You can obtain your free report by signing into the yearly credit report and following the bearings. At the point when you obtain your free report, it won't contain your credit score; however you can pay a little charge in the event that you might want to discover what your score is at the point at which you are requesting your free report. It is likewise highly recommended that you pull a report from every vault independently rather than every one of them together with the goal that you can question any mistaken information to every department independently. In the event that you report an issue to just one of the bureaus, it won't be fixed among every one of the three of the bureaus. Keep in mind the bureaus are independent of one another and have no correspondence among one another either. A few creditors report to just 1 authority, some report to 2 bureaus, some report to every one of the three bureaus, and some don't report to any. This is the reason you should ensure that you check every one of the three credit repositories when you are using your free yearly credit report. All in all, your credit is important and understanding the nuts and bolts of how your credit scores are obtained is similarly as important.

Chapter 2: What's a Good Credit Score?

In the present current economy, its a lot harder to qualify for a loan. Presently you need an excellent credit score to qualify for most types of credit. So what's a good credit score rating?

850 is immaculate credit and the most elevated credit score rating conceivable; however, I've never personally observed anybody with a 850. A good credit score begins in the 670 territory. Scores lower than 670 are not viewed as good credit.

Understanding FICO Credit Score

FICO Scores are one of numerous elements almost all lenders in the U.S. think about when they settle on key credit choices. Truth be told, a US News and World Report article expressed that "The FICO Score is the No. 1 bit of information to decide the amount you'll pay on a loan and whether you'll get credit." Such choices incorporate whether to endorse your credit application, what credit terms to offer you, and whether to expand your credit limit once your credit account is built up. FICO Scores are utilized by a huge number of creditors including the 50 biggest lenders, making it the most generally utilized credit score. At the point when you acknowledge new credit and oversee it tenaciously by reliably paying as agreed, you show to lenders that you speak to a good credit hazard. Lenders utilize your credit history as a method for assessing how well you have dealt with your credit till date.

A FICO Score is a three-digit number determined from the credit information on your credit report at a customer reporting agency (CRA) at a specific point in time. It outlines information in your credit report into a solitary number that lenders can use to survey your credit chance rapidly, reliably, unbiasedly and fairly. Lenders utilize your FICO Scores to assess your credit hazard— that you are so prone to pay your credit commitments as agreed. Also, it causes you obtain credit dependent on your genuine acquiring and repayment history without thought of disallowed types of information, for example, race or religion. Your FICO Scores from every agency might be diverse on the grounds that FICO Scores depend exclusively on the particular credit information in that agency's credit file, and not all lenders report to each of the three CRAs. Indeed, even in occurrences where the lender reports to each of the three CRAs, the planning of when information from credit grantors is refreshed to your credit file may make contrasts in your score over the three CRAs.

Notwithstanding the three-digit number, a FICO Score incorporates "score factors" which are the top factors that affected the score. Tending to a few or these score variables can assist you with improving your monetary wellbeing after some time. Having a good FICO Score can place you in a superior situation to qualify for credit or better terms later on.

FICO Scores are utilized by lenders regarding a wide assortment of credit Items such as:

- Credit Cards
- Auto Loans
- Personal Loans & Lines of Credit
- Student Loans
- Home Equity Lines & Loans
- Mortgages

How FICO Scores Help You

A FICO Score gives lenders a quick, objective and predictable gauge of your credit risk. Prior to the utilization of scoring, the credit allowing procedure could be moderate, conflicting, and unjustifiably one-sided. Here are a few different ways FICO Scores help you.

Get credit quicker

FICO Scores can be conveyed immediately, helping lenders accelerate credit card and loan endorsements. This implies when you apply for credit, you'll find a solution all the more immediately, even inside seconds. Indeed, even a home loan application can be endorsed a lot quicker for borrowers who score over the lender's base score necessity. FICO Scores likewise permit retail locations, web locales, and different lenders to make "moment credit" decisions. Remember that FICO Scores are just one of numerous factors lenders think about when settling on a credit decision.

Credit decisions are more attractive

Utilizing FICO Scores, lenders can concentrate on the realities identified with credit risk, instead of their genuine beliefs or inclinations. Factors, for example, your sexual orientation, race, religion, nationality and conjugal status are not considered by FICO Scores. So when a lender utilizes your FICO Score, it is getting an assessment of your credit history that is reasonable and objective.

More established credit issues mean less

In the event that you have had issues covering tabs previously, it won't frequent you everlastingly (except if you keep on taking care of tabs late). The effect of past credit issues on your FICO Scores blurs over the long haul and as ongoing great installment designs appear on your credit report.

A Higher FICO Score sets aside you cash

At the point when you apply for credit – regardless of whether it's a credit card, a vehicle loan, an individual loan or home loan – lenders need to see how risky you are as a borrower so as to settle on a decent decision. Your FICO Scores may influence not just a lender's decision to concede you credit, yet in addition, how much credit and on what terms (interest rate, for instance). Remember that FICO Scores are just one of numerous factors lenders think about when settling on a credit decision.

A higher FICO Score can assist you with fitting the bill for better rates from lenders—most times, the higher your score, the lower your interest rate and installments. The contrast between a FICO® Score of 620 and 760, for instance, can be a huge number of dollars over the life of a loan.

Think about these two models:

Two unique individuals are getting $230,000 on a 30-year contract. A borrower that has FICO Score of 760 could pay $211 less every month in interest in contrast to a borrower with a FICO Score of 630. That is an investment funds of $75,960 over the life of the loan.

On a $20,000, 48-month automobile loan, the borrower with a FICO Score of 720 could pay $131 less every month in interest as compared to a borrower with a FICO Score of 580. That is a reserve funds of $6,288 over the life of the loan.

How to Obtain a Good Credit Score:

There are five criteria that your credit is scored upon which are rather simple to follow.

1. The Payment History accounts for 35% of your credit score. Do you pay your bills on time? If that you don't do anything else yet make timely payments, you will have a good credit score in two years. Clearly, staying away from new assortments, court activities, and most effectively late pays will support your credit. Past wrongdoing assumes the biggest job in harming your credit score. One ongoing multi day late payment will bring down your credit score, in all probability by 20! A few late payments and your score will drop extremely far, exceptionally fast. multi day lates hurt your score considerably more, and multi day lates are a main problem. Know that the later the wrongdoing, the more negative the impact on your score. One multi day late a month ago will sting more than even a multi day late 4-5 years prior (5-10). Make sure to remain over your debt. Take alert to make timely payments and deal with accounts before they are late or go to assortment. Try not to overextend yourself so that it harms your odds of making timely payments. If that you have old late pays that can't be questioned off your credit report, realize that time heals old injuries and your score will increase given that no new

misconducts are reported. Pay before the Grace Period placed on your Credit Cards. Creditors charge extra expenses for late payments. This is an exceptionally enormous benefit place for a bank. Presently, not exclusively is there a due date. However, there is likewise a due time. A bank may charge a $30-$35 expense for being 2 hours late on your payments! (be sure to look at the fine print all things considered) Also, numerous banks have actualized under multi day effortlessness periods, abbreviated from 30 days, to increase overdue charges. Try not to sit tight for the due date! Get your payments in fast or pursue automatic charge payments on the web.

2. Amount Owed accounts for 30 Percent of your credit score. The credit scoring model determines credit balance, usually against your high credit limit. This is calculated in rates. It's imperative to keep your balances as low as could be allowed. In the event that you have a card with a $5,000 credit limit, keeping your balance beneath $500 places you in the 10% scope of accessible credit. There are thresholds in debt proportion that will make your credit score bounce higher. These thresholds are 70%, half, 30% and 10%. If that you can't pay off your credit cards the whole distance, pay them down BELOW the following conceivable edge. Calculate your credit limits along these lines. In the event that you have a card with a $5,000 limit, increase 5000 x.10

(or .30, .50, .70) You will need to pay your balance underneath these sums. For this situation - under $500 (or $1500, $2500 or $3500). Keep in mind; the principal activity is to check your credit report for credit limits. If that your high limit isn't reporting, the scoring model will utilize your balance as your credit limit. This implies you're utilizing 100% of your availability. Call your creditor and make sure they right it. Conveyance of debt is a simple method to make sure you keep up a solid score. Attempt to have a good spread of debt with lower balance to limit proportion. For instance, its better to possess $2,000 on 5 cards than it is to possess $10,000 on a card with others paid off. In case you're knocking up towards your credit limits, apply for more credit, or request an increase in credit from your current accounts. This criteria depends on all out availability, not estimate of availability. It doesn't make a difference If that you acquire $500 or $50,000. It's the means by which you handle it that issues. Disseminating debt onto extra cards or credit lines can assist you with raising your score rapidly.

3. The Length of Credit History counts for 15% of your credit score.
Length of credit history implies to what extent you've had your credit accounts. If that you've had a record for 15 years, it is more grounded than a having another record open for

just two months. An important hint here is to never close your credit cards. Keep your old accounts open in the event that they are in good standing, regardless of whether you don't utilize them and there's a zero balance. Keep in mind, however; you do need to utilize your credit lines something like clockwork. Accounts unused for 6 months become idle and are overlooked by the credit bureaus, except if there is a reprobate action joined to that record. Keeping your credit lines open likewise helps in improving your credit availability, clarified in the past segment. If that looking to include credit, ask your card organization to increase your credit limit. The best spot to increase your credit lines, beside getting another card, is to broaden your line on an old record with a good long history. Be sure they report the credit amount increment to the bureaus accurately. A normal factor of amazingly good credit scores are long credit narratives. Credit reports that possess old accounts with a fifteen to twenty year history are probably going to have a lot higher scores. It is, nonetheless, conceivable to add an old tradelines to your credit report.

4. Amount of New Credit accounts for 10 Percent of your credit score

A new credit implies fresh out of the box new accounts as of late open. You do need to begin some place, yet construct gradually. In the event that you have recently applied for 10 credit cards, banks will, in general, accept the likelihood that possibly you've lost your employment and are needing a back up plan. Attempt to begin with one little credit extension and work from that point. Make sure that you can deal with the payments reliably, are rarely late, and keep your balances as low as could be allowed, or totally paid off.

5. Kind of Credit utilized accounts for 10% of your credit score. The credit scoring model loves to see that you have an assortment of types of credit in your file. The absolute best arrangement of credit is to have a loan on a home, a vehicle payment and a couple of credit cards. This credit is spread crosswise over various types of lenders and sort of credit reached out to you. There are a couple of types of credit to avoid. Payday loans are terrible spots to have credit with and your scores endure a shot for having these types of high risk loans. Other very awful types of credit are the offers that enable you to have no payments for a year. These are hazardous, on the grounds that the conditions of the understanding may incorporate that in the event that you don't pay the loan off in a year, on day 366 you will owe the whole years worth of payments at normally 20% interest. This is a debacle already in the works. Individuals who more than once go for these offers are individuals who fall into

credit difficulty. You ought not have that sort of credit on your credit report.

There are a few things to consider when one is contemplating what is a good credit score. One method for evaluating the capacity of a borrower to pay back a loan is to see that person's credit score. The scores can be high or low or in the center. In the event that a score is high, at that point it is accepted that a person would have the option to obtain significant credit and can without much of a stretch pay back assets loaned to them. If that a score is low, the recognition is the inverse. A low score will make lenders careful, and it won't be simple for one to have monies stretched out to them. In a lender's eyes, different scores may mean various things, contingent upon the sort of scoring framework that specific creditor employments. This important credit score one obtains is useful to those choosing whether or not to loan reserves. Those substances expanding credit can make sense of the amount of cash to offer an individual and with what interest rate also.

Credit scores are made out of a varying level of numbers, somewhere in the range of 300-850. A score is made up of a range of appropriate factors. A gander at the payment history information comprises of thirty-five percent of the score. Watching the amount a person owes is 30%. The credit history life span is fifteen percent of the score. New spending information creates 10%. Thought of the different sorts of credit utilized is the staying 10% of the score number.

Equifax, Experian, and TransUnion are three understand credit reporting offices. One free yearly credit report can be obtained from every one of these organizations for an absolute check of three reports per year. It is important to process the substance that are on one's report with extreme attention to detail. Information that isn't accurate and right can sometimes be found. Sometimes errors in late payment content, payment chronicles, and amounts of monies owed can be seen. A person can be sure in looking into the report that there is no wholesale fraud also.

Substances expanding credit will be cautious in taking a gander at numbers on a person's credit scores. Generally, lenders feel that a score of 700 or above is believed to be awesome to fantastic. One would esteem keeping their scores high due to the numerous preferences of conditioning a high credit number. Credit expansions with low interest rate offers would be verified by the high scoring report proprietors. Additionally, fast credit endorsement procedures can be gotten by those with that superb high score!

In the rundown underneath, one can see the incentive in glancing through the eyes of a credit lender to take in the information as they see it:

Astounding credit is a score of 760 or above. Generally, excellent credit is an indent beneath with that 700 to 759 score. A good score falls in the range of 680-699. An alright score is 620-679. A fair or not terrible, but not great either number is summarized in the 580-619 section. If that a score lies in the 300-579 territory, the score is viewed as inadequate.

It is imperative to the individual needing credit to scrutinize their report roughly 6 to 12 months before applying for a major loan. In checking the report and seeing the score, one can search for any errors and make sure subtleties are recorded accurately. This time outline permits a credit searcher the chance to start a procedure of making amendments where required if errors were found. If that errors still show on the report at the time of applying for an enormous loan, one must tell the lender of these slip-ups.

There is the likelihood to improve one's credit score. This should be possible in observing that monies owed are routinely paid, diminishing extraordinary record balances. Since timeliness of payments is noted on each report, it is essential to make payments on time. It would be in the borrower's wellbeing to not assume new debt.

To finish up, there are a couple of pointers to remember in looking to get a good credit score:

- Credit advisors are accessible to help in an emergency money related position where payments can't be made. Likewise, the creditors themselves are undoubtedly ready to help in any capacity they can, including bringing down and spreading out payments. It is worthwhile to chat with creditors and credit advisors.

- Credit card balances must not be allowed to soar. Keeping up low balances is the key.

- A few people may figure it savvy to close old accounts to attempt to conceal any late payments shown on these accounts. It isn't reasonable to believe that shut accounts will improve one's credit score. Regardless of whether a record is shut, the late payment history will keep on showing on the credit report.

- Those loaning cash want to see a credit history with dynamic obtaining that returns quite a long while or more.

- Sharp bits of knowledge and cautious thought will come approach to accomplish what is a good credit score range. Accomplishing this will come route in your personal financial life.

Finding out your Rico scores

You can buy your FICO Classic scores separately for $15.95 (each score accompanies the credit report from which it is determined), or you can buy every one of the three scores and credit histories one after another for $47.85. To make a buy, go to www.myfico.com and click on "Shop." Then look down to "FICO Deluxe" to buy every one of the three scores and reports, or to "FICO Standard" to buy only one score. After you pay for your buy utilizing a significant credit card, you'll get moment online access to your score(s) and report(s).

At the point when you buy at least one of your FICO scores, you'll additionally get a clarification of the different factors, both positive and negative, that affected your score(s), access to the FICO Score Simulator—which you can use to calculate how your score(s) will be affected If that you pay off a debt, open another record, etc—and tips for what you can do to increase the scores. If that you have inquiries regarding your Classic FICO scores or the Score Simulator, call 1-800-319-4433, the client service number for myFICO.com. It's a good plan to order each of the three of your three FICO scores at regular intervals and audit them alongside your credit histories. Do the equivalent two or three months before you apply for important credit, protection, business, etc., so you will have the opportunity to clear up any issues in your credit files that may be lowering your credit scores.

Tips for raising your FICO scores

In the event that your Classic FICO scores are in the pits, don't surrender. You can accomplish a few things to raise them, for example, the accompanying:

- Regularly audit every one of your credit files for errors, fragmented information, and outdated information, all of which can lower your credit scores. In the event that you find any of these issues, get them adjusted as quickly as could be allowed.

- Stay alert for signs that your personality has been taken. If that a character criminal opens new credit accounts in your name, defaults on the accounts, or runs up your current accounts, your credit scores will be harmed.

- Pay your debts on time. On-time payments are the most ideal approach to improve your Classic FICO scores. The more drawn out your history of on-time payments the better, so in case you're behind on any of your accounts, get made up for lost time as quickly as possible.

- Pay down the exceptional credit balances you can find on your credit cards. You get closer to your credit limits as your balance increases, the more harm you're doing to your credit scores. Additionally, accelerate the rate at which you pay off installment loans, for example, vehicle loans.

- Don't manage high credit card balances by moving the debt starting with one credit card then onto the next so as to exploit lower interest rates. Rather, center around paying off those debts.

- Only apply for credit that you only need. Indeed, even one application for new credit will lower your Classic FICO to some degree.

- Don't close old accounts, regardless of whether you never use them, and they have zero balances. The Classic FICO scoring model considers to what extent you've had credit. Indeed, having a great deal of credit accounts harms your scores, however, once you have them, your scores have just endured a shot.

How Credit Scoring Came into Being

The question remains: How did one minimal number come to have such an outsized impact on our lives? Credit scoring has been in far reaching use by lenders for a very long while. Before the finish of the 1970s, most significant lenders utilized some kind of creditscoring recipes to choose whether to accept or dismiss applications. Many were acquainted with credit scoring by two pioneers in the field: engineer Bill Fair and mathematician Earl Isaac, who established the firm Fair Isaac in 1956. Throughout the years, the pair persuaded lenders that scientific recipes could make a superior showing of foreseeing whether an applicant would default than even the most experienced loan officials. An equation wasn't as dependent upon human impulses and inclinations. It wouldn't turn down a possibly good credit risk on the grounds that the applicant was "an inappropriate" race, religion, or sex, and it wouldn't accept a terrible risk in light of the fact that the applicant was a companion. Credit scoring, helped by perpetually incredible PCs, was additionally fast. Loaning decisions could be made in merely minutes, as opposed to days or weeks. Right off the bat, each organization had its very own credit-scoring equation, customized to the amount of risk it needed to take, its history with different types of borrowers, and the kind of individuals it pulled in as clients. The factors that nourished into the recipe shifted, however many considered the applicant's salary, occupation, length of time with a business, length of time at a location, and a portion of the information accessible on their credit report, for example, the longest time that a payment was ever overdue.

The Difference Between Credit Scores & Credit Reports.

You can't turn on Tv or use the web without seeing or hearing a promotion about getting your credit score. The credit score is essentially a number that addresses a present appraisal of your credit history that is contained in your credit report. Creditors use the score to pick quickly in case you are likely going to repay an account or loan, without having to deliberately study the credit report on which it is based. in the event that your score is high, you are most likely going to be offered credit at good rates. in the event that your score is underneath the creditor's edge for routine support, it might charge you higher rates or costs or reject you.

You in all probability, have more than one credit score. an arrangement of associations use their own one of a kind conditions to look at credit reports and think about their own appraisal models. A couple of associations offer a wide range of scores for different uses and different creditors. Likewise, those credit scores can change after some time, improving or progressively lamentable. Since credit scores are based upon your credit reports, impressively knowing what is in your credit reports is more important than knowing your credit scores. In case you need an unrivaled credit score, you need to monitor what is in your credit report.

Your Credit Report

Credit reports are articulations made by credit reporting agencies about a consumer. Reports may incorporate information about a consumer's credit value, credit standing, credit limit, character, general notoriety, personal attributes, or method of living.

A few creditors will review your credit report legitimately, others may just review a credit score using your report, and others may review both your credit report and at least one of your credit scores. Credit reporting agencies are generally revenue driven organizations that assemble and sell information about a person's credit history. They get a large portion of the information they collect about you from your creditors.

Practically all creditors supply information about their accounts utilizing a standard electronic reporting framework. You may hear it alluded to as "Metro 2." it has a number of "fields" (that is, boxes or spaces) in which the creditor may embed data about your credit and you. Credit reporting agencies turn around and sell off the credit information they have collected from an assortment of creditors and different sources to banks, mortgage lenders, credit associations, credit card organizations, retail establishments, vehicle vendors, debt collectors, insurance agencies, proprietors, and businesses. These organizations and people utilize the credit information to enhance applications for credit, protection, lodging, and business. Credit reporting agencies may likewise give distinguishing information and credit reports to government agencies for their utilization in broadening credit, reviewing the status of an account or endeavoring to collect a debt, giving a permit or other advantage, or exploring global psychological warfare.

Here are three across the nation credit reporting agencies:

- Equifax (www.equifax.com)

- Experian (www.experian.com)

- TransUnion (www.transunion.com)

There are additionally local and small credit reporting agencies, a significant number of which get their information from one of the three across the nation credit reporting agencies. At long last, across the country, forte reporting agencies accumulate and report just specific types of information, for example, terrible check composing or rental or medicinal histories.

Getting Your Credit Report

Getting a duplicate of your credit report is a fundamental piece of credit fix. Regardless of whether your credit is solid, you ought to get and review your reports once consistently. Under the Fair credit reporting act, credit reporting agencies that collect and keep up les of open record information and credit account information about consumers across the nation are required to provide you a free-of-charge copy of your credit report like clockwork, in the event that you request it. You can likewise review a sample report on a few of the credit reporting agencies' websites.

Forte credit reporting agencies (clarified beneath) likewise should provide you with a free report like clockwork, in the event that you request it and there are approaches to get extra credit reports in specific conditions or to pay for a credit report.

Getting a Sample Credit Report

In the event that you don't have any desire to get your own credit report yet, you can get a sample report to vet. For what reason would you need to hold back to get your report? To get your own credit report, you need to provide the credit reporting agency with personal information, including your address. in the event that debt collectors or creditors don't have your present address and it's not yet available in your report, you may not wish to make your address known. All things considered, you can see a sample credit report on the websites of Experian and TransUnion. For Experian, go to www.experian.com, click on "credit training," at that point "credit reporting," at that point, "my credit report" and pursue the connection in the article to see a sample credit report. For TransUnion, go to its training site, www.truecredit.com, look down and click "sitemap," at that point, click "Sample Single credit report." Equifax's sample is practically indecipherable, so don't mess with it.

Obtaining Your Free Credit Report from equifax, experian, & transUnion:

To obtain your free report from any or every one of the three across the country credit reporting agencies (Equifax, Experian, or TransUnion), contact the yearly credit report Service.

Here's the secret:

- go to www.annualcreditreport.com

- place a phone call at 877-322-8228, or

- Use mail at annual credit report request Service, P.o. Box 105281, atlanta, ga 30348-5281.

If you obtain your report online, you will need to input your state as well as some of your information, such as your date of birth, full name, social security number (you can check the box instructing the agency not to include the first five digits of your Social Security number on the report it provides you as protection against identity theft), previous addresses and current address, if you've been at your immediate address less than two years.

The annual credit report Service will then ask you to choose which of the three nationwide credit agency reports you want. Choose any one. The Service will then send you to the website of the company, and you'll have to provide answers to some security questions (such as, how much is your mortgage payment?). Note the reference number of your report so you can later access and print it if you need to correct errors later.

Don't get intimidated if you are bombarded with advertisements for additional services (such as paying for a credit score or credit monitoring). Just obtain your annual credit report for which there is zero charge. If you prefer, you can write or call to request a copy of your credit report.

How to Fix your Credit Score Report Errors

Among other things, the Fair Credit Reporting Act requires both the banks and merchants credit and the reporting agencies that provide them with data to correct inaccurate or incomplete information in your report when it's pointed out to them and can be proven. By law, once you request a correction from a credit bureau, it must respond within 30 days. Normally, the credit bureau will take your correction or complaint to the company that you believe has made an error and ask them for additional information. If you have proof that an error was made, you can expedite things by providing it to both the bureau and the company you are complaining about. It is critical you do this work with all three bureaus when you find an error. Fixing an error at Equifax won't correct it at Experian or TransUnion. They are all separate companies that compete with each other, and they do not share information.

All three credit bureaus recommend you use the correction forms on their websites, rather than sending in your complaint via regular mail. But if you feel more comfortable sending them a registered letter than relying on an online form, here is a sample letter you can use as a model.

(The mailing address of each bureau is listed afterward.)

[Insert Date]

[Insert Name of Credit Agency]

[Insert Address]

RE: Request to correct errors in credit report #[insert your credit report's file number.]

Dear [insert agency's name]:

In reviewing the credit report you sent me on [insert date], I have noticed the following errors:

1. [Describe the first error—e.g., "You list my date of birth as Jan. 1, 1900."] This is incorrect. The correct information is: [be very specific here and accompany it with proof if you

have it—e.g., "As the enclosed copy of my birth certificate shows, my date of birth is July 25, 1963."].

2. [Describe the second error—e.g., "You list me as having an active charge account with Sears."] This is incorrect. The correct information is: [be very specific here and accompany it with proof if you have it—e.g., "I closed this account on March 15, 2001. Please note the enclosed copy of the letter I sent Sears instructing them to close the account."].

3. [Describe the third error—e.g., "You list me as having made two late payments on my Bank of America home mortgage."] This is incorrect. The correct information is: [be very specific here and accompany it with proof if you have it—e.g., "I have made all my mortgage payments on time. Please note the enclosed copy of my latest mortgage statement as well as a letter from Bank of America confirming this fact."].

On the report of the Fair Credit Reporting Act, you are required to respond to my request within 30 days. My contact information is: [insert your mailing address and phone number].

Sincerely yours,

[Insert your name]

A 10-Step Action Plan to improve your credit score

The basic truth is that raising your score isn't that difficult If that you realize what to do. It's principally a matter of understanding the factors that FICO and the credit bureaus gauge and afterward making sense of which of them you can improve. As I said previously, I've instructed actually a great many individuals on fixing their credit scores, and based on that experience, I've built up a 12-advance activity intend to get your score up quickly and keep it there. I guarantee you—paying little respect to where you are beginning from, in the event that you pursue this arrangement, in six months, your score will be higher than you suspected conceivable.

1. Get your credit report and scan it for errors.

I clarified before how basic errors are in credit reports and that it is so natural to get them revised. When you get your report from www.annualcreditreport.com, experience it with extreme attention to detail and bring any harming errors you may discover (for instance, late payments that were really paid promptly or credit limits that are lower than they ought to be) to the consideration of the credit agency by sending them an affirmed letter. Be informed that, under the Fair Credit Reporting Act, the credit reporting agencies are required to address inaccurate or deficient information in your report inside 30 days after it's indicated out them. (Every so often, errors can support you, as when accounts you shut are recorded as being open; don't feel obliged to address these.)

2. **Automate your bill-paying, so you never miss a cutoff time.**

This might be the most important hint. Missing payments—even only one—can truly hurt your credit score. Consequently, I firmly suggest that you utilize your bank's online bill-paying support of automatically move a pre-set amount each month from your financial records to cover at any rate the base payments on the entirety of your credit accounts. I personally have each and every bill of mine "automated" along these lines. Therefore, I never need to stress over being late on any payment, regardless of whether I am voyaging.

3. **If that you have missed payments, jump on it and get current.**

It's never past the stage where it is possible to get it together. Get yourself updated as quickly as you can and afterward stay current. Your score will start to improve inside a couple of months — and the more you keep it up, the more perceptible the increase will be. The negative weight FICO provides for awful conduct like wrongdoings reduces after some time, so as long as you stay on an honest way of life, those dark imprints will eventually vanish from your record for good. Be that as it may, recollect—late payments can stay on your record for as long as seven years—so get those bills paid on time. The sooner you get a record of paying, at any rate, the essentials, the better.

4. Keep your balance well underneath your credit limit.

Of the considerable number of factors you can control—and improve quickly—the amount you owe is likely the most dominant. What makes this particularly important is that as far back as the credit crunch initially hit in the fall of 2008, credit card organizations have been cutting clients' credit limits all of a sudden. As indicated by one banking expert, the amount of credit accessible to consumers through credit cards and other credit lines has been sliced down the middle as of late—from an aggregate of $5 trillion toward the start of 2008 to simply $2.5 trillion toward the finish of 2010. On a personal premise, this can be annihilating to your credit score. Let's assume you have a $1,000 balance on a card with a $2,000 credit limit—and afterward, the card organization slices your limit to $1,000. All of a sudden, you've gone from half credit usage to being pushed to the limit, which can shave 45 from your credit score. The credit bureaus prescribe that you keep your utilization beneath 33% of your accessible credit. Since there's nothing you can do to ensure your score, if a credit card organization decreases your limit self-assertively, it's essentially important to keep your credit usage as low as conceivable consistently.

5. Be careful with the credit card transfer game.

For a considerable length of time, individuals have been setting aside cash by transferring high-interest credit card balances to low-interest cards. This can, at present, be useful, yet know that utilizing one credit line to pay off another sets off credit-score alerts—regardless of whether everything you're doing is combining your accounts. Every other thing being equivalent, your credit score will be higher If that you have a lot of little balances on a number of various cards instead of a major balance on only a couple.

6. If that you rack up high balances, pay your credit card bill punctually.

"Amounts Owed" section of your credit score is based on the balance due recorded on your latest credit card explanations. So irrespective of whether you pay your bills in full every month, running up high balances can at present hurt your score. You can stay away from this issue by paying down all or part of your bill before the finish of your announcement period, along these lines decreasing the balance due that will be documented with FICO and the credit bureaus.

7. Hold tight to your old accounts, regardless of whether you're not utilizing them.

A section of your credit score is based on to what extent you have had credit accounts. Closing old accounts abbreviates your credit history and diminishes your all out credit—neither of which is good for your credit score. In the event that you need to close an account, close a generally new one and keep the more established ones open. Additionally, closing an account won't expel a terrible payment record from your report. Shut accounts are recorded directly alongside dynamic ones.

8. Utilize your old cards.

In the fallout of the credit critical point, the credit card industry has gotten considerably more severe about closing inert or inactive accounts. This can affect your credit score since it decreases the average age of your credit accounts. To prevent this from transpiring, pull out your old cards and start putting in any event one charge on every one of them consistently. This will keep the account open, which thus will keep your credit history pleasant and long—and at last, raise your score.

9. Demonstrate that you can be capable.

The most ideal approach to raise your score is to demonstrate that you can deal with credit capably—which implies not acquiring excessively and paying back what you do get punctually. Don't nor create new accounts just to increase your accessible credit or make a superior assortment of credit. This is valid if you are simply starting to set up a credit history. Including a ton of new accounts may look risky—and it will reduce the average age of your accounts, which can, however, hurt your score If that you don't have quite a bit of a reputation. You should open new credit accounts just if and when you need them

10. At the point when you're shopping for a loan, do it quickly.

At the point when you apply for a loan, the lender will "run your credit"— that is, send an inquiry to one of the credit-rating agencies to discover how creditworthy you are. An excessive number of such inquiries can hurt your FICO score since that could demonstrate you're attempting to obtain cash from various sources. Obviously, you can generate a ton of inquiries accomplishing something superbly sensible—like looking for the auto loan or best mortgage by applying to a number of various lenders. The FICO scoring framework is intended to take into consideration this by considering the length of time over which a progression of inquiries are made. So attempt to do all your loan shopping inside 30 days, so the inquiries get clumped together and it's conspicuous to FICO that you are loan shopping.

Know the difference between a "soft inquiry" and a "hard inquiry."

Fair Isaac and the credit bureaus all recognize the difference between you checking your own score (what is called a "soft inquiry") and the banks or lending organizations checking your score (a "hard inquiry"). While a lot of hard inquiries can lower your score, soft inquiries don't count against you at all. So, it is okay to review your credit score as often as you want.

Consider buying a 3-and-1 Report as well as a credit-monitoring package and identity-theft service.

I am constantly urging my readers not to sign up for unnecessary monthly expenses. That said, I really do think that your credit score and your credit report are so significant that it makes sense to pay for a 3-and-1 Report (which provides you with your credit scores from the three big bureaus) as well as an identity theft monitoring service. Any of the three credit bureaus will sell you a 3-and-1 Report for roughly the same price. And all of them now offer Identity Theft Monitoring Programs. Most likely, these services will cost you around $14.95 and $19.95 a month, depending on the company.

Chapter 3: Credit Scoring Myth

For a large portion of credit scoring's history, by far, most of the people engaged with loaning decisions pretty much needed to think about what hurt or helped a score. Makers of scoring formulas would not like to uncover much about how the models functioned, for dread that contenders would take their thoughts or that consumers would make sense of how to beat the framework. Luckily, today we discover much increasingly about credit scoring—however, not every person has stayed aware of the latest knowledge. Mortgage intermediaries, loan officials, credit agency agents, credit guides, and the media, among others, continue to spread outdated and out and out bogus information. Following up on their terrible guidance can put your score and your accounts at critical risk.

Here are probably the most widely recognized fantasies.

Myth 1: Closing Credit Accounts Will Help Your Score

This one sounds sensible, particularly when a mortgage merchant discloses to you that lenders are suspicious of people who have heaps of unused credit accessible to them. All What's you, all things considered, from hurrying out and charging up a tempest? Obviously, looking at the situation objectively, what's shielded you from piling on huge balances before now? In the event that you've been pretty responsible with credit before, you're probably going to continue to be pretty responsible later on. That is the essential standard behind credit scoring: It rewards practices that show moderate, responsible utilization of credit after some time, in light of the fact that those propensities are probably going to continue.

The score likewise rebuffs conduct that is not all that responsible, for example, applying for a lot of credit you don't require. Numerous people with high credit scores locate that one of only a handful hardly any detriments for them is the number of credit accounts recorded on their reports. At the point when they go to get their credit scores, they're informed that one reason their score isn't considerably higher is that they have "too many open accounts." Many mistakenly expect they can "fix" this issue by closing accounts. In any case, after you've opened the accounts, you've done the damage. You can't fix it by closing the account. You can, however, make matters more awful.

Closing accounts can hurt you in two different ways:

- Closing down accounts can make your credit history look more younger than its actual age. Your credit score puts into consideration the age of your most recent account and the average age of every one of your accounts. So closing accounts, particularly more recent accounts, can ding your score.

- Closing accounts decreases the complete credit accessible to you, making your debt use proportion take off. Remember that the FICO equation gauges the gap between the credit you use and your all out credit limits. The more extensive the gap, the better. In the event that you all of a sudden lower that limit by closing down accounts, the gap limits—and that is a terrible thing.

This is genuine whether you keep a balance on your credit cards or pay them off in full each month. Remember: The FICO equation doesn't separate between balances that are taken and those that are paid away. As a general rule, closing revolving credit accounts can never support your score, and it may hurt it.

Sometimes the change was fairly self-evident, for example, a negative imprint that spent the seven-year limitation and was dropped from the report. All the more frequently, the distinction in scores was the consequence of something subtler, for example, lower balances being documented on the borrower's accounts or the straightforward overdue of time. (keep in mind that: The prolonged it's been since you created your first account and your last account, and the longer you've been paying on time, the better the impact on your score.) This doesn't imply that you should never close a credit card or other revolving account. You should dispose of a card that is charging you a yearly expense or shut down a couple of unused accounts to decrease the chances they could be commandeered by a character hoodlum. In the event that your FICO score is as of now in the mid-700s or higher, you ought to be fine closing a couple of accounts—insofar as they're not your most established or highest-limit cards. Something else, however, you'd be brilliant just to leave those accounts open until your score improves.

There are other good motivations to close accounts. Provided that you have a genuine spending issue, you may discover cutting up and dropping your credit cards is simply the best way to keep in line. In the event that that is valid, your credit score is presumably the least of your stresses. You additionally may experience one of those lenders who is scared by open credit card accounts and requests that you close a few. If that the loan is enormous enough, similar to a mortgage, and the lender has just dedicated to giving you the cash, you may need to go for broke to get your loan. However, don't close accounts as a precautionary measure and hurt your credit score.

Myth 2: You Can Increase Your Score By Asking Your Credit Card Company to Lower Your Limits

This one is a minor departure from the possibility that decreasing your accessible credit by one way or another enables your score by making you to appear to be less risky to lenders. By and by, it's missing the goal. Narrowing the difference between the credit you use and the credit you have accessible to you can negatively affect your score. It doesn't make a difference that you requested the decrease; the FICO formula doesn't recognize lower limits that you mentioned and lower limits forced by a creditor. All it sees is less difference between your balances and your limits, and that is not good. If that, you need to enable your score, to handle the issue from the opposite end: by paying down your debt. Expanding the gap between your balance and your credit limit positively affects your score.

Myth 3: You Can Hurt Your Score Through Checking Your Own Credit Report

By the myth about closing accounts, the myth that you can hurt your score just by checking your credit report is by all accounts the most unavoidable—and conceivably dangerous. You have to inspect your credit report and your score fairly habitually to make sure all is directly with your financial world. Checking once a year is about the base; given the commonness of data fraud, you should check in with every one of the three bureaus, in any event, two times every year. You should pull every one of the three reports and scores a couple of months before applying for new credit since it can take for a spell to address any errors you find. The people at Fair Isaac comprehend your need to review your very own information, which is the reason the FICO formula ignores any inquiries generated when you check your very own reports and scores.

Where you can hurt yourself is in the event that you request that a lender check your score. At the point when a lender pulls your credit, it generates what's known as "hard" inquiry—and those are meant something negative for your score. For whatever length of time that you order from a credit agency or a help subsidiary with an authority, for example, MyFico.com, your inquiries won't hurt your score.

Myth 4: You Can Damage Your Score By Looking Around for the Best Rates

The people spreading this particular myth may have a ulterior rationale. All things considered, If that you don't know what the challenge is offering, by what means will you get to know whether you got a good bargain? Makers of scoring formulas realize that savvy consumers need to shop around for the best rates, particularly on vehicles and homes. That is the reason the FICO formula ignores all mortgage-and auto-related inquiries made inside the past 30 days. If that the formula finds any inquiries before that period, it irregularities together any auto-or mortgage-related ones made inside a specific period. (More seasoned variants of the FICO formula utilize a 14-day period, while more up to date forms use 45 days.) as a result, in the event that you had six mortgage inquiries and three auto inquiries inside that time outline, the formula would tally just two inquiries all out. So in the event that you do your shopping for a vehicle loan or mortgage in a particular period of time and get the loan before the 30-day window is up, you ought to be fine. Regardless of whether it takes a little longer than 30 days to get your loan endorsed, as regularly occurs with mortgages, you ought to be alright if your rate-shopping was kept to a fourteen day period.

What you don't have any desire to do is drag out the procedure more than a little while or apply for credit cards directly before you intend to get a mortgage or a car loan. The "deduplication" process—that is the thing that Fair Isaac calls it—just gives unique treatment to inquiries that are car-or mortgage-related. You'd likewise be savvy not to shop for car loans while you're searching for a mortgage, or the other way around, since the formula irregularities mortgage and auto inquiries separately. You can ensure yourself further and make the shopping procedure simpler by doing some examination before you contact any lenders. Get your reports and scores with the goal that you know where you stand, and afterward check Internet destinations, for example, MyFico.com or Bankrate.com, to see the kind of rates you can hope to get, given your score. That way you'll have the option to tell a good arrangement from a terrible one when it's advertised.

Incidentally, talking about terrible gives, you ought to be careful not to give any credit or other personal financial information to a car business until you're prepared to buy the car. Perusers have reported discovering many inquiries on their credit reports subsequent to having coolly visited a business or two. Albeit different inquiries made around the same time probably won't affect your score that much since they're altogether lumped together by the FICO formula, a page of inquiries may alarm any lender who really takes a gander at your report. People who have poor credit should be particularly careful about inquiries. Despite the fact that somebody who has a good score may lose 5 or so from a single inquiry, the impact can be more prominent for somebody who has a beset, meager, or brief credit history. More than once, going after for loans and being turned down can negatively affect your score over the long run.

Myth 5: You Don't Need to Use Credit for You to Get a Good Credit Score

A few people are so suspicious of credit that they exhort surrendering credit cards and living on a money just premise. They recognize that a great many people need mortgages and auto loans, yet they feel the most ideal approach to dazzle a lender is by carrying on with a credit-free life.

Since you know something about how credit scoring functions, you can see the gaps in this hypothesis. The credit scoring formula is intended to pass judgment on how well you handle credit after some time; in the event that you have no credit, or you don't in any event sometimes utilize the credit you have, the formula won't have enough information to make an evaluation. You don't need to live in debt to get a good score, yet you do need to utilize credit. Previously, a few people had the option to get high credit scores without having a lot of credit. Prior incarnations of the FICO credit score gave scores more than 700 to certain people with only a couple of as of late opened accounts.

The recent forms of the formula, notwithstanding, make it a lot harder to get a grandiose score If that you have a slender credit history. You most likely should be worried about your score regardless of whether you have no designs to take out loans. Since back up plans are utilizing credit information for endorsing and rating decisions, your inability to keep up a credit history could cost you as higher premiums. It's really awful that faithful people who basically don't care for debt ought to be rebuffed with higher premiums, and a few states have even prohibited guarantors from utilizing an absence of credit history as motivation to raise rates. If that your state hasn't precluded the training, however, you should tidy off your credit card and use it sometimes.

Myth 6: You Need to Pay Interest to Obtain a Good Credit Score

This is the precise inverse of the past myth, and it's similarly as misinformed. It is not necessary for you to carry a balance on your credit cards and pay interest to have a good score. As you've perused a few times as of now, your credit reports—and subsequently the FICO formula—make no differentiation between balances you carry month to month and balances that you pay off. Savvy consumers don't carry credit card balances under any circumstances, and absolutely not to improve their scores. Presently, the facts confirm that to get the highest FICO scores, you have to have both revolving accounts, for example, credit cards, and installment loans, for example, a mortgage or car loan. What's more, except for those 0 percent rates used to drive auto deals after Sept. 11, most installment loans require paying interest.

Yet, here's a news streak: You don't have to have the highest score to get good credit. Any score more than 720 or so will get you the best rates and terms with numerous lenders. A few, particularly auto and home value lenders, save their best bargains for those with scores more than 760. You don't must have a 850, or even 800 score, to get incredible arrangements. In case you're attempting to improve a fair score, a little, reasonable installment loan can help—provided that you can get affirmed for it and pay it off on time. However, some way or another, there's no motivation to stray into the red and pay interest.

Myth 7: Addition of a 100-Word Statement to Your File Can Aid Your Score

If that You Have an Unresolved Dispute with a Lender Dave in Los Angeles ended up in an extended battle with his telephone organization, which for quite a long time charged him for a telephone line that, truth be told, never worked. He went all around with the organization's specialized help, client assistance, and charging department. At last, he quit any pretense of, declining to pay the bill—in any event, when it went into collections and to his credit report. Dave found out he could counterbalance the damage to his credit by sending the credit bureaus a 100-word proclamation clarifying the issue. Government law gives you the privilege to have such statements connected to your credit file. Tragically, the credit scoring formula can't peruse—at any rate, not in the customary sense. It calculates scores based on how things on your credit report are coded, and these 100-word statements aren't coded by any means, so they're not checked. It's not clear how accommodating such statements were before credit scoring turned out to be so across the board, yet they're surely very little help now.

Given how harming late payments, collections, and other ongoing negative marks are on your score, you need to stay away from them if at all conceivable. This doesn't really mean you need to give in and pay a bill that is plainly in mistake. However, you likewise shouldn't let a $30 spat with your book club escalate into a collection that could junk your score. You may need to pay the bill under dissent and afterward sue the seller in little cases court. Luckily, most credit debates can be illuminated well shy of that. If you utilized a credit card to buy something that didn't work, you can utilize the credit card organization's contest goals process as sketched out on the back of your statements. Quiet, pleasant steadiness with an organization's client assistance department can likewise help, as can a readiness to search out directors or controllers who may have the option to slice through a log jam.

Myth 8: Your Closed Accounts Should Indicate "Closed By Consumer," Or They Will Hurt Your Score

The hypothesis behind this myth is that lenders will see a closed account on your credit report and, if not educated generally, will accept that a nauseated creditor cut you off in light of the fact that you botched in some way or another. Obviously, as you most likely are aware at this point, numerous lenders never observe your real report. They're simply taking a gander at your credit score, which couldn't care less who closed a credit card. Fair Isaac figures that if a lender closes down your account, it's either for dormancy or in light of the fact that you defaulted. If that you defaulted, that will be sufficiently archived in the account's history. In the event that it makes you feel better to contact the bureaus and guarantee that accounts you closed are recorded as "closed by consumer," by all methods do as such. However, it won't make any distinction to your credit score.

Myth 9: Credit Counseling Is Way Worse Than Bankruptcy

Sometimes this is expressed as "credit advising is as awful as bankruptcy" or "credit directing is as terrible as bankruptcy." None of these statements is valid. A bankruptcy recording is the single most noticeably terrible thing you can do to your credit score. On the other hand, the current FICO formula totally ignores any reference to credit guiding that may be on your credit report. Credit guiding is treated as an impartial factor, neither aiding nor hurting your score. Credit guides, in the event that you're inexperienced with the term, have practical experience in arranging lower interest rates and also working out payment plans for debtors that may some way or another file for bankruptcy. In spite of the fact that credit advisors may consolidate the consumer's bills into one monthly payment, they don't give loans—as debt consolidators do—or guarantee to wipe out or settle debts for not exactly the chief amount you owe.

The fact that credit guiding itself won't affect your score doesn't mean, notwithstanding, that enrolling in a credit advisor's debt management plan will leave your credit sound. A few lenders will report you as late only for enrolling in a debt management plan. Their thinking is that you're not paying them what you initially owed, so you ought to need to endure some agony. That is not, by any means, the only way you could be reported late. Not all credit instructors are made equivalent, and some have been blamed for retaining consumer payments that were proposed for creditors. The missing payments comes as "lates" on the consumers' credit reports, hurting their scores.

Credit advising isn't something you should pursue since you need a lower interest rate or one spot to send your payments rather than many. However, in case you're behind on your debts or ready to pay just the essentials, and you need an option in contrast to bankruptcy, you shouldn't stay away as a result of myths regarding its long-term impact on your credit.

Myth 10: Bankruptcy Can Damage Your Score So Much That It's Impossible to Get Credit

Bankruptcy deals an overwhelming hit to your score; however, that doesn't mean you can't get credit a while later—or even that you'll need to hold up that long. You can get a mortgage in as meager as six months after your bankruptcy is released (finished). You may get credit card offers before your case has even closed. How quickly you'll restore credit and the amount you'll pay for it will depend to a great extent on your conduct after you file for bankruptcy. In the event that you start taking care of credit capably—paying your bills on time, not running up huge balances, and not applying for a lot of credit on the double—your score will start to recuperate.

In any case, it likewise will matter which lenders you approach for credit. Most standard lenders evade people who have filed for bankruptcy—sometimes only for the initial hardly any years, albeit sometimes for whatever length of time that the bankruptcy stays on your file. Different lenders represent considerable authority in what's known as "subprime" borrowers—those with not exactly consummate credit, including bankrupts. You'll must be careful on the grounds that some subprime lenders charge outrageous rates and expenses. Be that as it may, you in all likelihood will have the option to get the loans you need in the event that you search.

Chapter 4: Credit Bureau

Credit bureaus are privately held, billion dollar organizations whose primary reason for existing is to make cash; that is what revenue driven organizations do right? They keep data that lenders furnish them - regardless of whether accurate or inaccurate - about our credit association with them and sell it. Basic right? This straightforward plan of action generates over $4 Billion per year!

One wellspring of income for them originates from selling the information on our credit reports to different lenders, managers, insurance agencies, credit card organizations - and whoever else you approve to see your credit information. In addition to the fact that they provide them with crude data; yet they likewise sell them various methods for examining the data to decide the risk of stretching out credit to us. In addition to trading our information to lenders, they likewise sell our information to us - credit scores, credit observing administrations, extortion security, wholesale fraud prevention - interestingly enough this region has quickly gotten perhaps the greatest wellspring of income. Furthermore, those pre-endorsed offers in our letter drop each week; or garbage mail? That's right; they got our information from the credit bureaus as well. Organizations buy in to an assistance provided by the three credit bureaus that sell them a rundown of consumer's credit information that fit a pre-decided criteria.

Presently, as opposed to prevalent thinking, credit bureaus don't have any contribution on whether you ought to be endorsed for a loan or not; that is absolutely based on the credit criteria of the lender you're working with. However, by utilizing the entirety of the information that has been set on your credit report (personal information, payment history, and credit propensities) and FICO's technique for scoring that data, they do tell them with how creditworthy you are.

Origin and History of Credit Bureau

In recent decades credit has gotten easier and easier to obtain. Credit cards, for example, were once given basically to the wealthier classes in the public eye and were utilized just once in a while. Toward the start of the twenty-first century, practically 50% of all Americans had in any event one broadly useful credit card (that is, a Visa, MasterCard, American Express, or Discover card). The ascent of credit as a typical method to buy necessities, extravagances, and everything in the middle of implies that credit bureaus process more information and are a more crucial part of the general economy than any other time in recent memory. Credit bureaus likewise monitor and investigate the data got from a regularly expanding number of loans for homes, cars, and other high-cost things.

Today, credit bureaus consistently accumulate information from creditors (banks; credit-card guarantors; mortgage organizations, which have practical experience in loaning cash to home buyers; and different businesses that stretch out credit to people and businesses) and amass it into files on singular consumers and businesses, while refreshing their current files. In addition to the data gathered from creditors, credit files may likewise contain one's business history, previous addresses, false names, bankruptcy filings, and removals. Information usually remains on a credit report for seven years before being evacuated.

The greater part of the nearby and provincial consumer credit bureaus in the Untied States are claimed by or are under agreement to one of the three essential consumer credit-reporting administrations referenced previously. Every one of these three organizations assembles and appropriates information separately, and credit scores and reports vary somewhat from bureau to bureau. Each organization keeps up around 200 million singular consumer credit files. Frequently a lender will utilize an average of the credit evaluations provided by the three unique bureaus when choosing whether or not to make a loan.

The basic business credit bureau in the United States is Dun and Bradstreet. D and B has credit files on more than 23 million associations in North America and on more than 100 million businesses around the globe. In addition to giving creditors information important to decide a credit applicant's capabilities, credit bureaus make their data accessible for progressively questionable purposes. For example, standard mail advertisers regularly buy information from credit bureaus as they continued looking for potential clients. If that you have ever gotten a letter revealing to you that you have been pre-endorsed for a particular credit card at a particular yearly percentage rate, it is valid; the credit-card organization definitely realizes your credit rating and has to be sure previously affirmed you for the predefined card. Forthcoming managers and proprietors sometimes buy credit histories, as well.

What Credit Bureaus Do?

Credit bureaus collect information from various sources in accordance with consumer information. The activity is done for various reasons and includes data from singular consumers. Included is the information concerning a people charge payments and their getting. Utilized for evaluating creditworthiness, the information provides lenders with an outline of your accounts if a loan repayment is required. The interest rates charged on a loan are additionally worked out concerning the kind of credit score shown by your experience. It is thusly not a uniform procedure, and your credit report is the significant instrument that affects future loans.

Based on risk based valuing, it pegs various risks on the various customers in this manner deciding the cost you will acquire as a borrower. Done as credit rating, it is an assistance provided to various interested parties in the public. Terrible credit histories are affected for the most part by settled court commitments which mark you for high interest rates every year. Duty liens and bankruptcies, for example, shut you out of the conventional credit lines and may require a great deal of arrangement for any loan to be offered by the bank.

Bureaus collect and examine credit information including financial data, personal information, and elective data. This is given by various sources generally marked data furnishers. These have an exceptional association with the credit bureaus. An average gathering of data furnishers would comprise of creditors, lenders, utilities, and debt collection agencies. Pretty much any association which has had payment involvement in the consumer is qualified including courts. Any data collected for this situation is provided to the credit bureaus for grouping. When it is accumulated, the data is placed into specific repositories and files claimed by the bureau. The information is made accessible to customers upon request. The idea of such information is important to lenders and managers.

The information is in this manner material in various conditions; credit evaluation and business thought are simply part of these.

The consumer may likewise require the information to check their individual score and the home proprietor may need to check their inhabitants report before renting an apartment. Since the market is saturated by borrowers, the scores will, in general, be robotic. Straightforward examination would deal with this by giving the client a calculation for speedy appraisal. Checking your score once every other year should deal with errors in your report.

Individuals from the public are qualified for one free credit report from every one of the significant bureaus. Business reports, for example, Paydex might be gotten to on request and are chargeable. Lawful expressions for the credit bureaus incorporate credit report agency, CRA in the US. This is organized in the Fair Credit Report Act, FCTA. Other government rules associated with the assurance of the consumer incorporate Fair and Accurate Credit Transaction Act, Fair Credit Billing Act and Regulation B. Statutory bodies have additionally been made for the regulation of the credit bureaus. The Fair Trade Commission serves to as a controller for the consumer credit report agencies while the Office of the Comptroller of Currency fills in as a manager of all banks going about as furnishers.

Three Major Credit Bureau

The most ideal approach to manage your credit capably and assume responsibility for your financial circumstance is to be educated. This takes a brief period and exertion on your part, yet since your credit scores are so important to dealing with your accounts and setting aside cash, it's your duty to know as much as you can regarding the credit bureaus that formulate credit appraisals. To assist you with getting a running beginning on that strategic's, some information on TransUnion, Experian and Equifax, the primary credit bureaus in the U.S.:

TransUnion

TransUnion has workplaces the nation over that manage various parts of credit: credit management, identity theft, and other credit issues; and types of credit customers, for example, personal, business, and press inquiries. If that you discover errors on your TransUnion credit report, you can call them at 800.916.8800 or visit their site to debate them. If that you believe that you're a casualty of identity theft, call them at 800.680.7289 at the earliest opportunity.

Experian

Like other credit bureaus, Experian provides a wide range of various administrations for people, businesses, and also the media. Experian is based in Costa Mesa, CA, and has a website, yet in the event that you discover errors on your report or need to report a potential identity theft, this credit bureau makes it elusive telephone numbers on the site. Rather, they encourage guests to utilize online forms for questions, identity theft reports, and different issues.

Equifax

Based in Atlanta, GA, Equifax likewise has various departments to help people with various types of questions and concerns. Their website is additionally set up to have people utilize online forms to address errors, report identity theft, and handle different concerns. In any case, if somebody believes that their identity has been taken, the individual in question can, however, call 888.397.3742 to report it to Equifax. If that somebody detects a blunder on their Equifax credit report, that person must utilize the contact number on the report to question it. There is no number on the site to describe errors.

These are the 3 credit bureaus in the nation, and they each adopt an alternate strategy to enabling people to get in touch with them to pose inquiries or address any issues they might be encountering. Rather than reaching the credit bureaus legitimately, numerous people prefer to utilize a credit checking administration to assist them with dealing with their credit and stay over their funds. The credit bureaus all have comparative projects; however, most people prefer to utilize a free organization to assist them with these issues. That way, they get an impartial perspective on their credit score and a lot more devices to proactively manage and improve their credit ratings.

Chapter 5: Section 609

The best method for improving your credit score uses Section 609 of the Fair Credit Reporting Act. Segment 609 is an area of law that tells the credit bureaus and other reporting agencies precisely what they should do so as to make someone's debt information public.The 87 pages of this law comes down to two essential things. To begin with, the information they provide must be accurate. Second, that information must be undeniable.

Most credit fix organizations attack the initial segment of the law - the precision of the information. They have their customers pretend that the debts aren't theirs or get a second social security number to make a subsequent credit file - a strategy which is highly illicit, incidentally.

A legitimate credit rebuilding organization will accept it as a given that that the information on the report is accurate. They do this regardless of the way that measurements show that 25% of the information on credit reports is in mistake. It is a lot easier and increasingly effective to put the weight of evidence on the reporting agency to confirm the information - that is, they leverage the second part of Section 609. They do this since they KNOW that the credit bureaus are not lawfully or appropriately checking the information as required by the law.

In this way, it's expected everything in a credit report is 100% accurate. Furthermore, they know better. They realize that 25% of all credit reports have errors on them. The obvious side, be that as it may, is a completely unique story. Also, Section 609 is express about what verifies an account. The main snippet of information that verifies an account is a duplicate of the first documentation - for example, the first agreement between the debtor and the creditor. Rarely does a credit bureau have this documentation!

In this way, to fix your credit and improve your credit score, you simply need to compose a letter to the credit bureaus and request certain verification of the information on the report. If that they don't provide this inside 30 days, they have overstepped the law.

Reestablishing your terrible credit isn't a difficult activity. If that you are prepared, willing and have the persistence to manage the "delay and scare strategies" of the Credit Bureaus and provided that you have the correct step-by-step guidelines and the correct instruments to do it with. The connected "Segment 609 Legal Dispute Do-It-Yourself Letters and Instructions" are the best possible apparatuses to utilize. Don't let the straightforwardness of the letters and the frequently called "odd-ball" guidelines trick you. They work, despite the fact that the time that it takes to get constructive outcomes will vary from person to person thinking about that sometimes it might take 3 or 4 "adjusts" of sending the different letters we give you in the package yet eventually these letters will drive the credit bureaus to expel the pessimistic things that you request them to.

So as to see how and why this package will empower you to get the entirety of your negative things removed from your credit reports, you have to comprehend a smidgen about the credit reporting business. There are three principle Credit Reporting Agencies alluded to as CRA's and/or credit bureaus. They are Equifax, Experian and TransUnion.

At the point when you engage in a credit exchange (loan, mortgage, credit card and so forth.) with a bank or some other creditor the information for every one of these accounts will be reported to at least one of these CRAs (credit bureaus) by every creditor and every month each "credit thing" will be reported in your "credit file" which is recorded under your social security number, physical address, and full name.

The Fair Credit Reporting Act was placed into law before the electronic and computer age. Despite the fact that the credit business has been attempting to campaign Congress to re-write the law to fulfill current innovation guidelines note that the current form of the Fair Credit Reporting Act (FCRA) needs the CRA's to have physical duplicates in their files of documentation to help each account being reported on. It is additionally important to comprehend that the creditors report the entirety of your credit items to the credit bureaus electronically. They don't send duplicates of any physical reports at all to the credit bureaus. IMPORTANT: What that implies is that the credit bureaus don't review or potentially confirm any credit applications, marked contracts, or any archives at all before they report the thing on your credit report. They accept any credit items that a creditor sends to them electronically. They accept these credit items as "genuine" and right and belonging to you.

Every month your bank or creditor sends an "electronic file" with the subtleties of your account to every one of the credit bureaus.

o date of last activity;

o high credit o balance;

o account number;

o date opened;

o payment term o status (borrower, co-borrower, joint);

o historical status (as agreed, 30 days delinquent);

o payment amount;

o amount past due;

o customer information secured from the credit application.

What's more, the credit bureaus essentially place this information into your credit file with NO VERIFICATION done concerning whether the account is legitimate, the information is right or whether the creditor even has the privilege to report the thing on your credit report. Basically the three principle credit bureaus give the creditor the opportunity to be vindicated that they are reporting accurate information. For what reason would they give the creditors the opportunity to be vindicated you inquire?

The primary response to that question is on the grounds that the creditor pays the credit bureau to report the thing and the creditor likewise pays the credit bureaus each time they pull your credit report. The credit bureaus gain a huge number of dollars a year reporting everything without exception on your credit report that a creditor gives them.

Credit bureaus are a "for-profit" organization and they get paid to put items on your credit report and they get paid when these equivalent creditors pull your credit report. Creditors can charge you a higher interest rate, the more negative items that are put on your report. The problem with this strategy for reporting is that ANY CREDITOR can basically report anything they desire about you, whether it is right or not. There is a significant irreconcilable situation going on here don't you concur? The Federal Government saw a major problem with this technique for reporting so they believed that they tackled the problem when they passed what is known as the Fair Credit Reporting Act (FCRA). It should ensure you and I and administer the exercises of Credit Reporting Agencies and regulate how they report information about you. It sounds good in principle yet read on to discover why it isn't working.

If that you study this Federal law and furthermore study the case law built up in different court cases relating to different segments of the FCRA you will see that the FCRA necessitates that all Credit Reporting Agencies Are Supposed to VERIFY ALL INFORMATION got from creditors BEFORE this information is placed onto your credit file. Appropriate confirmation as indicated by set up case law includes the credit bureau having duplicates of the first marked credit application in their files.

They are required to have a duplicate of the credit application that you marked when you created the credit account with the creditor in their files. They should have it in their files to show that they checked the information and account is yours and to show that they confirmed the information before they set it on your credit report. The reality of the situation is ... the credit bureaus don't review any records, not to mention keep a duplicate of your credit application in their files. They NEVER see any documents. They don't want to see any documents.

NOTE: For individuals who have ever endeavored to read the FCRA (Fair Credit Reporting Act) to see where it expresses that the credit bureaus should have archives on file that verify the exactness of each account reported in your credit file I don't need to disclose to you that this government law like most laws leaving our United States Congress are "unintelligible". They are clearly composed by skilled lawyers paid by lobbyists taking a shot at benefit of the huge banks and the credit reporting agencies. Our congressmen and ladies who sit on the boards of trustees that draft up these laws clearly don't read the laws after they are composed by these lawyers to check whether the law that they drafted are composed the manner in which they drafted them. The FCRA law is about as simple to read as the expense code, don't you concur?

How It is Supposed to Work: For instance, how about we expect you are going to buy a car and fund that car. At the point when the Credit department of that car business subsidize an arrangement with a lender, the seller gives up the 2 most important financing archives: the agreement + the credit application. When the lender is happy with these and the essential supporting records, the lender subsidizes the loan. The lender presently has the duty of reporting this current consumer's file to the 3 credit bureaus.

The lender should send the credit application to the 3 credit bureaus to properly verify this is the right client. This check piece is important. It's important in light of the fact that the business needs to conform to the Patriot Act and other forced regulations to properly verify, by verifying a duplicate of the consumers Driver License, that the person marking the agreement + the credit application is the person that was properly distinguished. Likewise, the lender utilized this credit application as verification that the consumer gave the creditor the privilege to pull the consumers credit file and check on the person's activity, income, living arrangement, references, and afterward affirm the loan. The credit application is the confirmation piece.

The lender at that point, on a monthly premise, sends its colossal email clump file to the 3 credit bureaus for all of their loans. In this monster file, it contains the information on each consumer that has a loan with them. The lender sends precisely what you see imprinted on the credit bureau report. The sent information incorporates:

o account number;

o date opened;

o date of last activity;

o high credit o balance;

o payment term;

o status (borrower, co-borrower, joint);

o historical status (as agreed, 30 days delinquent);

o amount past due o payment amount;

o customer information secured from the credit application.

The problem is ... .Even however the law requires the credit reporting agency to verify each account it reports on before reporting on it, the truth of the matter is the lender never under any circumstance, ever, direct the credit application to the 3 credit bureaus! No lenders ever send the credit application along these lines; the credit bureau NEVER verifies any of this information. Rather than sending the CRA a duplicate of the credit application to be confirmed, the creditor removes the credit file of the consumer and the creditor verifies the information that the consumer puts on the credit application themselves. The verification procedure was done in reverse. The law needs the credit reporting agency to verify the credit information not the creditor. This being the situation, anything that is remembered for your credit bureau file can be evacuated in the event that you request the credit reporting agencies right to report the thing by constraining them to show you the confirmation of verification that should be in their files. You can effectively evacuate both substantial negative items just as invalid items along these lines.

As indicated by the FCRA, if a credit file will be reported on a consumer's report it must be properly checked by the credit bureau. Every thing remembered for a credit report has a verification piece... be that as it may, the bureaus never possess it. The FCRA reported that the bureaus are the ones that need to keep this verification on file despite the fact that the bureaus will attempt to instruct you to go legitimately to the creditor and request this information as opposed to approaching the credit bureau for the documentation. This isn't good thinking about the lender, a corrupt court representative, or a collection agency or debt buyer could report anything they want on your credit report trying to pick up leverage against you to collect on a supposed debt or to legitimize to you why they are charging you a higher interest rate. The Section 609 Credit DIY Dispute letters used to debate your negative credit items are coordinated towards the 3 bureaus, not the creditor.

WHY & HOW The Section 609 Credit Dispute DIY Letter Works.

Remember the time it takes to get them to expel the entirety of the things that you request will differs from person to person. A person may send letter #1 and get for all intents and purposes the entirety of the contrary items evacuated in under 30 days.

Someone else may send letter #1 and just get a couple of accounts expelled. Or then again a third person may send out letter #1 and get the credit bureaus standard refusal structure letter or their terrorizing forswearing letter (more on this later). Notwithstanding the outcomes you get, it is important to be tireless and persevering. If that after the first "round" of letter #1's there is as yet deprecatory information staying on your credit report then you essentially send the following letter that we give you in your package and underlining that it is your "second Written Request for them to send you duplicates of their obvious evidence that the account being referred to or have the thing erased according to area 609.

Eventually, you will locate that the entirety of your censorious accounts will start to vanish. For certain people, it happens quickly and is very simple and for other people, it tends to be a battle and take any longer. Why?

IMPORTANT: The explanation we found that the time it takes to get your disputed items expelled changes from person to person is on the grounds that most dispute letters never get read by a "real human." Try to get the letter read by a real human rather than a computer. Here's the manner by which it works:

At first your dispute letter goes to a human yet he/she doesn't read it. They just 'open' the envelope and afterward run the page or pages through a computerized scanner. The examining machine does an optical acknowledgment of the words in your letter. If that your letter is type composed, at that point the name of the creditor and the account numbers that you are questioning can be read by the computer and they are contrasted with the creditor name and the account numbers in your credit file and in the event that they coordinate, at that point the computer automatically sends you a structure letter expressing that "the account information has been confirmed". Wham bam case closed.

The vast majority give up after they get an answer from the credit bureau that expresses that they have confirmed the account to be accurate. That is anything but difficult to do right? Taking into account that you realize that the account belongs to you. The vast majority are expecting this credit dispute process not to work so they quit when they get this answer from the credit bureau. That is the thing that the credit bureaus need you to do. Never Quit! So the main thing is to make sure that your dispute letter gets dismissed by the computer and gave to a real live person. So how would we do that?

We essentially suggest that you hand-write in the creditors name and account numbers instead of type them in on your letter. Now writing this part of the letter doesn't ensure that the human who is going to look (see I said "look" not read) at your dispute letter is going to automatically erase the items that you are contesting in light of the fact that the person in question sees that you are questioning their "entitlement to report" not the exactness of the thing. Without diving into a mess of detail of the obligations and limitations put on workers at the credit bureaus and to cut a long story short its get the job done to say that these people need to manage a large number of files every day which implies that they can possibly put in no time flat per file If that they are going to make their share every day. So despite the fact that you got your dispute letter past the computer and under the control of a real live person, these people may even now overlook your letter and therefore get the computer to reply you with another type of "structure letter" we call the "Terrorizing Form Letter Rejection".

You may get a letter over from them that inquires as to whether you are working with a credit fix organization or whether you paid an organization to assist you with drafting up your dispute letter and they may request that you fill out a survey and send it back to them before they will review your dispute. Try not to FILL OUT ANYTHING and return it to them. Just Use the letters in this package.

These types of threatening reactions are intended to discourage you and additionally scare you into accepting that you are accomplishing something incorrectly and get you to abandon your dispute. Credit Bureaus don't care for it when consumers file disputes since it costs them time and cash to do it regardless of whether they simply mail you back a "dismissal structure letter". They get countless letters a day which translates into a huge number of dollars to manage them. The sooner they scare you away or discourage you away the better it is for their benefits.

In the extraordinary situation where the CRA's attempt to overlook your numerous composed requests, you can decide to file a lawsuit and sue the CRA for damages under the Fair Credit Reporting Act (FCRA) and additionally file a conventional grumbling with the Federal Trade Commission (www.ftc.gov) for infringement of the FCRA.

Step-By-Step Instructions:

Under Federal Law, once every year – you can get a FREE credit report from every one of the three fundamental Credit Reporting Agencies.

CHECKING YOUR CREDIT REPORT

Personal Information

Check to guarantee that all personal distinguishing information is right, for example, your complete name, address, social security number (when disclosed), and birth date. Note if there are any varieties toward the start and anyplace else in the report (particularly in the segment held for address and name confuses, around the end). Minor name or address befuddles are common, for example, incorrect spellings or oversights of parts of names, for example, center names or hyphenated names. Deficient or incorrectly spelled addresses, wrong apartment numbers or postal codes are likewise common.

If that you locate any huge personal distinguishing information that is totally unrecognizable to you, make a note of the dates connected with these varieties. This could demonstrate that another person with comparative information to yours has previously applied for credit, and additionally these are simply errors that should be removed. In extraordinary cases, unrecognizable personal information joined with unrecognizable accounts implies that somebody may have utilized your identity or social security number to open new credit accounts.

Credit and Trade Lines

Output your credit and trade lines carefully. Search for the accompanying:

- Accounts you don't recognize.

- Negative or reprobate information. This incorporates late payments, statuses (on time versus reprobate, open versus come up with all required funds, and so on.) collections, charge-offs, decisions, liens, and bankruptcies. If that you've left any unbound credit card debts unpaid for over six months, at that point your accounts past the 180-day late imprint may change over to charge-offs. This implies the creditor has charged off the debt from its books and chose it is probably not going to get any kind of payment on the debt. Likewise be mindful of very late versus extremely old critical information.

- Any cosigned or shared services. Affirm your status on these.

- Inaccurate balances. Check that your most extreme charged or passable balances on revolving accounts are right.

Note where they are inaccurate. Remember that most lenders or banks report 30 days falling behind financially, so in the event that you've made any ongoing and critical payments to decrease balances this action may have not yet posted. Note: If your name is fundamentally the same as another person's in your family, for instance, your dad is Bob Jones Sr. also, you are Bob Jones Jr., now and again your credit data might be combined. While innovation and reporting has improved here as of late, this is as yet a common event, and any errors ought to be revised.

Inquiries

While reviewing your credit report, guarantee that you recognize the latest credit inquiries. Pay particular consideration by searching for any hard pulls that you don't recognize in light of the fact that these are the types attached to applications for new credit. Guarantee that the inquiries showing are in fact yours.

Likewise, search for any inquiries from more than two years back. These can generally be removed upon request.

If that you don't recognize the organizations by either names or addresses, at that point, you reserve a privilege to dispute them and have them removed. An unapproved inquiry without your express request or consent is an infringement as indicated by the FCRA.

Crosscheck Your Reports

Contingent upon which techniques you used to obtain your report, you may have one tri-blend report that has consolidated every one of the three CRAs' records, or you may have separate information crosswise over three single reports. In the two cases, decide if negative information is reported by only one CRA instead of the other two, and the other way around. Any disparities like these over the different CRAs ought to be hailed. Since you've parsed through your credit report, If that you've found your credit report to be accurate altogether, Congratulations! If at that point, we should work to remove any negative or inaccurate information you found. It is important to comprehend that sometimes you might be effective at removing negative information showing on your credit report irrespective of whether it is yours. This process is point by point in the following area, which incorporates presenting a composed dispute and goals request with the likelihood that the negative information can be removed.

The Dispute Process

In 2013, a report by the Federal Trade Commission evaluates that one out of each five people has an inaccurate credit report. On a national scale, that translates to upwards of 42 million missteps. In the event that you wish to remove negative items from your credit reports, you'll have to pursue the dispute goals request process. Requests are made in a formal composed process, in which you will submit letters to the CRAs or creditors expressing which negative items you wish to have removed from your credit reports. From the time of the receipt of the letters, the CRAs have 30 days to make a move. If that you find wrong information, you'll pursue a similar process, either requesting an expulsion of the thing (e.g., collection that isn't yours) or a redress (e.g., request that a late payment be adjusted to timely).

You may have gotten dispute letter forms included with your credit reports. For instance, here a sample dispute goals letter from TransUnion can be found on its website and at tccbonline.com. I've read that during the dispute process, you ought to provide as meager information as conceivable with respect to your personal and account information—you shouldn't reference the credit report ID or enclose a duplicate of the CRA's credit report, in light of the fact that thusly, you are just encouraging the reinvestigation process timeline. Driving the CRAs to begin from scratch with no information makes the multi day check tick faster in support of you, yet it's up to you. I've been fruitful at evacuations utilizing the two strategies.

Remember to stay sorted out during this process. You'll need to keep tabs on your development by keeping a worksheet of the trade lines being disputed, just as the dates when letters are sent. Keep duplicates of everything, and never send in unique duplicates of anything. From the time requests are made, the CRAs are required to react or remove negative and inaccurate information inside 30 days.

Reinvestigation and Reverification

The proper terms to request that negative items be removed from credit files are reinvestigation and reverification; however, these might be misnomers. These are terms utilized distinctly by the CRAs and those in the credit reporting ventures. They are basically equivalent to a standard examination and verification, however since credit reporting agencies believe any accumulating of a report to be an examination, they along these lines allude to the process of verifying that data as a reinvestigation.

Target Adverse and Negative Items

While the laws differs from state to state concerning legal time limit on credit report items, for some states most unfriendly information with respect to bankruptcies, collections, charge liens, decisions, some polite suits, and some kid bolster debts are on file for at any rate seven years. Hard inquiries stay on credit records for two years. All things considered, many have been fruitful at removing negative information from showing up at all on their credit reports, regardless of whether it was theirs.

"In any event, when a thing is accurate, dispute the information (if this is your course), since it costs nothing. There's constantly a chance that questioning sections can work," as indicated by Dana Neal in Best Credit. Sometimes, either due to broken record keeping or noncontact by a unique creditor or collection agency, the CRAs can't verify antagonistic items inside the allowed 30-day time outline; hence, naturally, they should remove them. This dispute process is the beginning stage to removing negative information, and many will find that they can do so effectively, utilizing the sample letters in this part, by having the CRAs remove the accompanying items from their credit report:

Bankruptcies: If endeavoring to remove a bankruptcy before the finish of the standard seven-year reporting period, you'll have a superior shot after at any rate two years from discharge, and after you've disputed and removed all debts that have a status showing they were incorporated under bankruptcy on the credit report.

Collections: If the bureau can't verify that the collection is genuine inside the reinvestigation time outline set out by the

FCRA (30 days), at that point the law requires that it be removed from your report. Collections are regularly reported by administration bureaus, which are famous for committing errors, including translating SSNs inaccurately; if the CRA can provide verification documentation, guarantee that it has recorded all information accurately since any errors are cause for cancellation.

Judgement: Attempt to dispute these; else you may need to arrange a settlement with the offended party. A paid judgment is far superior on a credit record than an unpaid one.

Tax Liens: While you might be fruitful in having a tax lien removed from your credit report with a standard dispute process, in the event that you really made good on the regulatory obligation lien in full and it was under $25,000, at that point late news demonstrates that the IRS might be pleasant in removing this item from your credit report. You may not charge so well if the tax lien is more noteworthy than this amount, and it is unpaid.

Inquiries: Hard inquiries ding your credit score. Dispute them to have them removed, particularly in the event that you don't recognize them. Remember that rate shopping, state in case you're attempting to get preapproved with a mortgage lender for another home, inside a 30-day timeframe won't ding your credit.

Prescreened offers likewise won't ding your scores, as these are viewed as delicate pulls.

Target Erroneous Items

In addition to questioning antagonistic items, you'll need to dispute negative items that aren't yours by any means. Whenever the situation allows, you'll need to provide proof, just If that it will address the item. Try not to mistake this for questioning antagonistic information, which concerns the whole erasure of a negative item. For instance, If that you have a credit card trade line showing a late payment that you need to dispute, you wouldn't have any desire to have the whole trade line removed from your report, as this is unreasonable; rather you'd simply need the late payment amended If that you have evidence of timely payment.

Tips for Your Dispute Letter

Dispute in Writing, Not Online

It's ideal to request your free yearly credit reports recorded as a hard copy to be delivered via mail from every one of the CRAs. In addition to the fact that this gives you a total picture of what every bureau has on file for you, yet it likewise prevents you from being dependent upon any limitations of obligation and mediation understandings that you should consent to while obtaining online reports.

Most online dispute forms give you simply enough room to express your dispute; however, don't give you enough room to back it up. Online disputes are likewise not set up to accept additional evidence, for example, a duplicate of your Social Security card or of a check, say specialists—and those bits of evidence can be important later If that you do need to go to court to prove that a credit reporting agency isn't amending a genuine mix-up. In addition, numerous online dispute forms contain mediation conditions, which can undermine your consumer rights.

Type up, at that point, mail your dispute. That way, you can incorporate as a lot of information and evidence as you have to clarify your case. Likewise, If that you do end up in court, you'll have the option to prove to the judge allocated to your case that you gave the credit bureaus enough information to properly explore your dispute.

Send in your dispute letters via mail. Better, send them by affirmed mail, or with delivery affirmation, so you can guarantee your archives were gotten. Keep duplicates of your dispute letter and all nooks. Compose the affirmed mail number on each letter so you can without much of a stretch match the ensured letter affirmation with the first dispute.

In the event that you have different items to dispute, don't attempt to dispute every one of them together. Contesting single items or close to two items one after another is the best practice, since, for instance, dispute letters that contain up to eight disputes at a solitary time may raise warnings and caution the CRA that you are in a ultra credit-cleanup mode, so don't cause to notice yourself. Rather, utilize the appropriate dispute template letter for close to two errors one after another. For additional disputes, mail those in separately on separate dispute letters. The probability of showing signs of improvement if the CRAs handle your disputes each in turn.

Make sure that If that you are questioning a negative item that is showing just on a solitary CRA's report, for instance, an account that is present on your Equifax report and not your Experian report, you send in the dispute letter to the right CRA. While the CRAs aren't committed to advise one another, I've read that they now and again speak with one another regarding inaccurate information to be removed. By and by, you wouldn't have any desire to bring on additional disarray or draw consideration structure the different CRAs to any information that is not currently there.

Send Your Letters to CRAs and the Original Creditor

In the event that you know which collection agency, lender, or other type of data furnisher (the ones giving out your information) is misreporting your credit history, send them a similar information that you sent the credit bureau. This method guarantees that data furnishers have enough information to research your dispute. According to the consumer lawyer Cary Flitter in the FBN report, "That is another motivation to do paper disputes since you will be trapped in the center." The credit bureaus process your dispute by doling out a classification code to the dispute and sending a short outline to the furnisher to research the problem. If that creditors don't respond, according to the CFPB website.

You can likewise log complaints with the Consumer Financial Protection Bureau. After we forward your complaint, the organization has 15 days to respond to you and the CFPB. Organizations are required to close everything except the most entangled complaints inside 60 days. You'll have the option to review the reaction and give us criticism. In the event that we locate that another agency would be better ready to help, we will advance your complaint and let you know. We likewise share complaint data with state and government agencies who supervise financial items and administrations, and we distribute a database of non-personal complaint information, so the public recognizes what kinds of complaints we get and how organizations respond.

Pursue the Formula

The best dispute letters are frequently the most effortless to read. Don't attempt to impel lawful contentions or utilize confounding, counterfeit legalese, or other extravagant expressions and words. Numerous letters that have been posted online as samples don't make sense, are ineffective and will accomplish nothing for you. Rather, a concise, pointed dispute letter that states considerately in plain English what the blunder is and what you need done about it is ideal. You should be clear about what you're contesting and are totally in your entitlement to state, "The account was rarely mine," or "The payment was rarely late." The letter must come straightforwardly from you, the consumer, to trigger credit bureau commitments for examination.

Include Evidence, Only If that It Helps

When sending in dispute requests, now and again, you'll need to include anything that evidence is accessible to help and back up your dispute. Obviously, in case you're contesting that the accounts or collections and negative information is yours by any stretch of the imagination, this administrative work won't be accessible. At the point when it helps your dispute, include documentation. For instance, in case you're questioning the reporting of a late payment, you'll need to include copies of monthly creditor account statements showing your payments posted in a timely way, starting with one month then onto the next without late charges.

Another case of supporting documentation could be copies of selections from your checking account statements, showing the dates of active bill payments, or whenever paid with check, a copy of the front and back images of the got the money for check. In the event that you managed anybody at the creditor concerning your issue, it generally helps to include an announcement typed out on a separate letter enumerating a particular dates, times, and with whom you talked at the organization. Another model would be in case you're attempting to address a status of a collection to Paid in Full. It is savvy to include the individual template letter in addition to verification of payment of the collection with the liquidated check copy just as any agency articulation for reference.

You're requesting that the CRA contact the original creditor or collection agency for verification, so provide what report as confirmation is accessible. Also, keep copies of everything as the CRAs and different parties may have lost parts of files and documentation. "A plethora of court cases on this turn on the degree of the information that the credit bureau gives the furnisher. The credit bureau will say, 'client claims paid,' yet they will never connect a copy of the check," says Cary Flitter, the consumer lawyer from the FBN report. The credit bureaus once in a while include the archives you mailed with your dispute (when they are reverifying); thus the furnisher just gets the absolute minimum of information. It's dependent upon you to have this information on the ready.

Chapter 6: Fixing Your Credit Score Fast

Credit bureaus have 30 days to examine complaints and frequently concede to what lenders state about you, regardless of whether it's valid. Regardless of whether all parties concur that a mistake has been made, the errors can continue to manifest in your file on account of the automated idea of most credit reporting. You may need to contact creditors and the bureaus a few times to get mistakes erased. The process may take weeks; best case scenario, you may be taking on the conflict for quite a long time or even years. In case you're amidst attempting to get a mortgage, these errors can cause significant problems. You probably won't have sufficient opportunity to fix your report before the house drops out of escrow or you stall out with an interest rate a lot higher than you have the right to pay.

Issues, for example, these might entice you to turn to one of the numerous organizations that guarantee "moment credit fix" or that assurance to help your credit score. No authentic organization makes such guarantees or certifications, however, so any individual who employs one of these outfits is asking to be misled. There are, in any case, a developing number of certified administrations that can actually fix your credit report errors in 72 hours or less. Read on to learn more.

Fixing Your Credit in a Matter of Hours: Rapid Rescoring

Rapid rescoring administrations came about in light of the fact that such a large number of people were losing loans or paying an excess of interest on account of credit bureau mistakes. Before you get energized, however, you ought to learn what these administrations can and can't do:

- They can't manage you straightforwardly as a consumer—Rapid rescoring is typically offered by little credit-reporting agencies, which fill in as a kind of go between the bureaus and the lending experts. These agencies, which are frequently free, however, which may be auxiliaries of credit bureaus, provide uncommon administrations for loan officials and mortgage representatives, for example, blended or "3-in-1" credit reports. To profit by rapid rescoring, you should work with a loan official or mortgage representative who buys in to an agency that offers the administration.

- They can help you just in the event that you have proof, or if proof can be obtained—Rapid rescoring administrations aren't intended to help people who presently can't seem to begin the credit-fix process. You need something in writing, for example, a letter from the creditor recognizing that your account was reported as late when you were actually reality on time. (This is one reason that it's so necessary to get everything in writing when you're attempting to fix your credit.) If you don't have such proof, however, the creditor has recognized the error, some rapid rescorers can get the proof for you. Nonetheless, that may add days or weeks to the process.

- They can assist you with getting errors fixed; however, they can't remove genuine negative things that are in dispute— Also, you need proof that a mistake was made—not simply your say as much. If that the credit bureau is already researching your complaint regarding the error, the item typically cannot be included in a rapid rescoring process.

- They can't vow to support your score—"How Credit Scoring Works," sometimes removing negative items can really hurt a score—strange as that may appear.

The scoring formula attempts to contrast you with people who have comparable credit histories. In the event that you've been lumped into the gathering with a bankruptcy or other dark spots on your report, you may find that your score falls when a portion of those negative items are removed. Rather than being at the highest point of the bankrupts' gathering, as such, you've dropped to the base of the following gathering—the people who have better credit. All the more commonly, removing an error probably won't help your score as much as you may have trusted and probably won't win you a superior interest rate. There are no assurances with rapid rescoring.

Be that as it may, Doug in Phoenix is one of the numerous borrowers who have profited up until this point. Doug filed for bankruptcy in 1998, yet a few of his cleared out debts were still displayed as open and unpaid on his credit report five years later when he applied for a mortgage. Technically, the accounts the sum total of what ought to have been reported as "included in bankruptcy." It's a popular enough error and one that can normally be fixed—If that you have a month or more.

Doug didn't. He stressed that he would lose the house he needed to buy and maybe pass up probably the most minimal rates borrowers had found in years. Doug's mortgage broker utilized his bankruptcy papers to prove the errors to a rapid rescoring service, which fixed the problems and supported Doug's score. The rate he got—a little more than 7 percent—was as yet higher than somebody who had good credit would have gotten at the time, yet it was obviously superior to the rate he may have gotten without the fix. This is actually the kind of mediation that the National Association of Mortgage Brokers was seeking after when it started campaigning in 1997 for an approach to accelerate the dispute process and keep old, proven errors from murdering mortgage bargains. Congress had made a few updates to the Fair Credit Reporting Act in 1996 that should support consumers; however, the problems stayed widespread.

Quite a long time ago, brokers and other lending professionals could take care of these problems. In the days prior to the widespread utilization of a credit score, a broker or loan officer could mediate to persuade a lender to disregard mistakes or little imperfections on a client's credit file. Everybody included comprehended that credit report errors were common, and having an accomplished loan pro vouch for your creditworthiness could frequently complete an arrangement.

With the coming of credit scoring and automated loan processes, however, those chances to advocate for clients quickly evaporated. Lending professionals shared consumers' dissatisfaction when incorrect information continued to be reported by the bureaus—information that frequently hosed credit scores and brought about more awful rates and terms than the borrower merited. The mortgage brokers needed an approach to slice through the bureaucracy and accelerate the process. Free credit reporting agencies, with their littler, specific staffs, started to fill the need. Here's the means by which it works. Your broker loan or officer obtains evidence from you that a mistake has been done, and he sends that proof to the credit agency that provides the rapid rescoring service.

The rescorers, thusly, have uncommon associations with the credit bureaus that enable their requests to be handled quickly. The rescoring service transfers proof of errors to unique departments at the credit bureaus, and the departments contact the creditors (typically electronically). In the event that the creditor concurs that an error was made, the bureaus quickly update your credit report. After that occurs, another credit score can be calculated. The expense for this service is typically somewhere close to $50 and $100 for each "trade line" or account that is remedied, albeit a few agencies provide the rescoring for no additional charge, as part of a part of services provided to lending professionals.

The presence of rapid rescoring does not change the way that you should be proactive about your credit. Months before applying for any loan, you have to order copies of your reports and start testing any errors. You likewise need to keep your correspondence about these errors. All things considered, rapid rescorers typically require some kind of paper trail to pursue to prove to the bureau that the mistakes in fact exist. In any case, If that you wind up highly involved with getting a mortgage and an old problem repeats, rapid rescoring can assist you with disposing of the problem and spare the arrangement.

All in all, how would you discover one of these services? In case you're already managing a loan officer or mortgage broker, ask whether she approaches a rapid rescoring service. If that your lending pro has never known about rapid rescoring—it's an ongoing enough advancement that some haven't—request that her contact the agency that provides her organization with credit reports to check whether it's accessible.

In case you're still in the market for a lending pro, make sure you ask about access to rapid rescoring. A portion of the online mortgage brokers, for example, Quicken Loan, additionally use rapid rescorers to support their customers. Imagine a scenario where you're not in the market for a mortgage, or generally don't qualify for rapid rescoring, however despite everything you need speedy outcomes. You'll need to rethink your meaning of snappy, first off. Barely any things are rapid in credit fix. The accompanying strategies typically won't show brings about 72 hours, however you may see a perceptible increase in your score in around thirty to sixty days.

Boosting Your Score in 30 to 60 Days

Rebuilding your credit can sometimes be an excruciatingly slow process, yet you can take a couple of easy routes that may increase your score in as meager as a month or two, as talked about in the accompanying segments.

Pay Off Your Lines of Credit & Credit Cards.

Probably the fastest approaches to support a score is to lower your debt use proportion—the distinction between the amount of revolving credit that is accessible to you and the amount that you're utilizing. One straightforward approach to improve your proportion is to redistribute your debt. In the event that you have a big balance on one card, for instance, you could transfer probably a portion of the debt to different cards. It's usually better for your scores to have little balances on a number of cards than a big balance on a solitary card. You additionally could explore getting a personal installment loan with your nearby credit association or bank, and utilize the cash to pay down your cards. Applying for the loan may affect your scores a piece; however, that is probably going to be more than offset by the development to your scores from lessening the balances on your credit cards. (Credit scoring formulas are substantially more delicate to the balances on revolving debt, for example, credit cards, than to the balances on installment loans.)

A riskier strategy may be to remove a 401(k) loan. These loans do not appear on your credit report; however, you do confront a big risk: If you lose your employment, you typically need to pay the cash back quickly, or you'll cause taxes and punishments on the balance. If you choose to take a 401(k) loan, make sure you'll have the option to repay the loan quickly to limit the risk.

Whatever you do, do not cash out a 401(k) or pull back cash from an IRA to pay off credit card debt. A couple of focuses' distinction on your credit score does not merit the short-and long-term costs you'll pay for a premature withdrawal. Albeit moving debt around can lift your scores, the best strategy for your numbers and your funds long-term is to pay off revolving debt—either out of your current income, utilizing cash that is sitting in a bank account, or selling stocks or different ventures, inasmuch as they aren't in a retirement account.

Utilize Your Credit Cards Lightly

A big difference between your balances and your limits is what the scoring formula likes to see —and it doesn't really care whether you pay off your balances in full each month or carry them from month to month. What makes a difference is the amount of your credit limits you're really utilizing at some random time. A few people demand they've supported their scores by paying off their cards in full a couple of days before their announcement closes. In the event that their credit card backers, as a rule, send out bills around the 25th, for instance, these people check their balances online about seven days prior and pay off whatever's owed, in addition to a couple of bucks to cover any charges that may manifest before the 25th. When the bills are really printed, their balances are pretty close to zero. (In the event that you utilize this method, simply make sure you make a second payment after your announcement shows up if your balance isn't already zero. That will make sure you don't get damaged with late charges—and truly, that can occur, despite the fact that you made a payment before in the month.) An easier method to hold your balances down is essentially to pay cash for most buys in the 3 months or so before you plan to get a loan.

Concentrate on Correcting the Big Mistakes on Your Credit Reports

If that another person's bankruptcy, collections, or charge-offs are showing up on your report, you will probably profit by having those removed. If that an account you closed is reported as open, then again, you'll probably need to disregard it. Having an account filed as "closed" on your file can't support your score and may hurt it.

Don't overlook a collection since it's little, or it's recorded as paid off. These are not kidding negative denotes that can fundamentally depress a credit score. In any case, don't get excessively irritated if the credit bureaus list an inappropriate business or incorrectly spell your center name. The credit scoring formula doesn't consider these details.

Utilize the Bureaus' Online Dispute Process

Some credit-fix veterans swear they get faster results along these lines, however regardless, you'll have to make printouts of all that you send to the bureaus and each correspondence you get from them.

Check whether You Can Have Your Creditors Update Positive Accounts or to Report

Not all creditors report to every one of the three bureaus, and some don't report reliably. If that you can get a creditor to report an account that is in good standing; however, you may see a quick knock in your score. Darren of New York had an extraordinary FICO score with Experian; however not out of the question scores with Equifax and TransUnion. The explanation? A large portion of his credit history was with a solitary credit association, and that credit association reported uniquely to Experian:

"Since mortgage lenders [use] the center score," Darren stated, "I am not getting the best arrangement since that isn't an accurate score."

The center score doesn't mirror Darren's full credit history. Darren hasn't had the option to persuade his credit association to report to the next two bureaus. That implies he's pretty much back to slow-path arrangements, for example, getting a installment loan or credit card from a lender that reports to each of the three bureaus and making on-time payments.

What Typically Doesn't Work

There's a great deal of folklore out there about how to fix a credit report fast. A large portion of it is false, for example, what's sketched out in the following areas.

Disputing Everything in Sight

A portion of the fake credit-fix places barrage credit bureaus with disputes about everything without exception. Previously, this may have been briefly effective if the credit bureaus removed the disputed items while they explored. Nowadays, however, the awful stuff typically stays on your file during the examination, so you don't get an impermanent lift. In any event, when you do, most or the entirety of the negative items essentially return directly when the original creditor affirms that they're right. What probably won't return are the accounts that are helping your score. The creditors probably won't try to respond to the bureaus' requests for affirmation, and you could wind up exacerbating the situation. Disputing such a large number of items without a moment's delay is likewise a good method to persuade credit bureaus that no doubt about it disputes, and they may decline to explore by any means. To play it safe, don't dispute more than three or four negative items without a moment's delay, except if (like Doug's bankruptcy accounts) your disputes are related. What's more, don't pay anybody a fat charge to do this for you.

Making "Another" Credit Identity

This is another most loved of trick specialists. They may have you utilize a dead newborn child's Social Security number or instruct you to apply for a taxpayer ID number, which the IRS typically issues to businesses. Regardless of whether you do manage to pull off this misrepresentation, you're left with a totally unfilled credit file. If that you believe it's difficult to get loans when you have pained credit, simply take a stab at getting credit with no history by any means. It could be years before you can qualify for OK rates and terms, and by then, all the negative marks you were so stressed over would have either tumbled off your original credit report or turn so old that they would scarcely affect your score.

Closing Troublesome Accounts

You can't get negative marks to tumble off any speedier by closing accounts, and you may twist up genuinely dinging your credit score. Misconducts, charge-offs, collections, and other negative marks can stay on your credit report for seven years, regardless of whether the original account is as yet open; bankruptcies can stay there for ten years.

Regardless of whether you've had problems with an account, it may at present be affecting your credit score. In the event that it's one of your more established accounts, it could be helping to make your credit history look pleasant and long—remember, more seasoned is better with regards to credit scoring. If that it's a revolving account, the credit limit is figured into your general debt use proportion. In the event that you close the account, you could make your current balances look bigger while making your credit history look more youthful than it is.

Chapter 7: Managing Debt

Your credit use rate or the aggregate sum of accessible debt utilized on your accounts (unsecured and secured) is the second biggest factor toward obtaining a solid credit score. Beside your verified debt, which is paid down according to a calendar and doesn't increase in the amount owed, we should concentrate here on uncollateralized debt, which is the most costly debt and furthermore, the debt that is least demanding to gain out of power. In case you're overpowered with debt, or have burrowed a huge gap from which you're uncertain how to begin moving out, my first advice is to unwind. There is absolutely no motivation to experience the ill effects of superfluous uneasiness or stress in light of debt. Losing rest and agonizing night and day over fortuitous debt won't assist you with receiving in return, so accept the way that you are in debt and start considering how and when you can receive in return.

CREDIT CARD DEBT IS THE COSTLIEST DEBT

Credit card debt is the most choking out debt of all, and the feeling of always digging and getting no place is a feeling to which I can relate very well. Don't give it a chance to make you crazy. With an activity plan and being persevering to not overextend yourself, you can gradually arrive at a point where your credit card debt is neither bringing you nor your credit score down. While I'm not a specialist in credit card debt guiding.

I realize that in my circumstance, I had the option to toss little lumps of my compensation at this pile of debt — a few months in bigger pieces, others in littler pieces—until I had a little enough balance to clear out. While this segment intends to provide some accommodating tips on the most proficient method to manage your debt, If that you believe you are absolutely up the creek without a paddle, or a significant life event, for example, joblessness, or a medicinal issue or anything is preventing you from having the option to pay down any of your debt, at that point jumping to the following segment might be progressively appropriate for you.

DEBT MANAGEMENT TIPS

For those of you who are in the limbo period of, "Should I pay-down debt," or "Should I file bankruptcy," comprehend that there are two types of personal bankruptcy: the main, Bankruptcy, takes into consideration most or the entirety of your debts to be discharged or dropped. The second, known as Bankruptcy, plans your debt for repayment over some stretch of time. If that you are thinking about both of the two choices, at that point it is highly recommended that you search out somebody with mastery, for example, a bankruptcy trustee or lawyer. Sometimes everything necessary is a professional's advice and helping hand to guide you the correct way. If you are going to attempt to dig yourself out of debt without documenting personal bankruptcy or choosing your debts for not exactly the aggregate sum owed with your creditors, you have to have a plan.

What's the Best Approach to Deal with Huge Credit Card Debt?

There is no uncertainty that the interest on credit card debt can be an executioner. Many credit cards have interest rates more than 20 percent. In the event that you utilize Chris' Debt Repayment Calculator (at welker.ca) you can perceive the amount it will cost to pay off your credit cards with interest more than five years. Perhaps the biggest error that people make when they are attempting to dig themselves out of debt all alone is making payments that simply spread the interest charges yet aren't really lessening the head.

Chris Walker says that If that you are battling to deal with your credit card debt and you need to pay back what you can bear, at that point the best alternative may be a consumer proposal for a repayment. By offering a consumer proposal, you can stop interest charges, prevent creditor collection activity, and settle your debt. While documenting a consumer proposal briefly damages your credit rating, it is frequently the best approach for people dealing with huge credit card debt. Don't make the mistake of concentrating on your credit rating. While credit rating is important, improving your financial wellbeing is undeniably progressively important. You can generally modify your credit rating, yet If that you don't have a plan to escape debt you will continue to battle.

If You Need to Manage Your Credit Card APRs

In cases of medical or employment hardships, or some other particular setbacks in life, creditors will sometimes permit a decrease or freeze on additional fund charges to your existing debt. Everything necessary is calling to discover what they can do subsequent to disclosing to them your circumstance—it might be critical enough to accommodate their explanation codes or extraordinary programs. Creditors frequently save these for people who might be not able make timely payments or the full amount of the average monthly payments due, and the programs may keep going for set time periods of six months to a year or more.

In return for enrolling in these programs, a few creditors may likewise stop your account preventing you from making additional buys and adding to your existing debt. Obviously, you won't realize what options you have until you call, so in case you're reluctant about grabbing the telephone, discover the time to call every one of your creditors and examine these options which could bring some truly necessary help. Inquire as to whether you can make a lesser monthly payment. This would be your most solid option If that you are as yet ready to manage a smidgen of a monthly payment, notwithstanding any plans for a DIY debt settlement. You'll be happy you called — anything to help diminish the amount of interest charged and APRs consistently. The goal here is to get what, assuming any, options you have, at managing or keeping your balances low. Twofold check that by enrolling yourself in any diminished APR or APR-freezing programs, creditors will continue reporting to the CRAs that you are making timely payments. (Creditors can begin reporting harsh payments if a bill is 30days overdue.)

Settling Your Own Debts

While personal debt settlement was to a great extent a totally unbelievable practice as meager as five years back, a plenty of DIY debt pilgrims have now taken their accounts of the process to online media and web journals. More news and research on the subject, by and large, has additionally now put the process inside go after the individuals who wish to take the creditors head-on. Many have picked this course to be in all out control of their settlement process as opposed to enlisting an outsider debt arbitrator to intercede. You can settle your debts all alone; anyway you should be prepared and solid willed. You'll need to suffer and confront creditors' and debt collectors' endeavors and strategies at getting you to pay up, which can be out and out forceful and smooth. Furthermore, you will must be sorted out at managing and monitoring the results of each arranged account. People are procured by organizations to make debt collection their full-time exertion and are compensated accordingly, so don't overlook they are professionals at endeavoring to get anything they can out of any debtor.

Debt settlement is positively an option for any individual who basically can't make payments or who has fallen so behind that the subsequent stage would resort bankruptcy. An outline of personal debt settlement includes:

1. Halting any payments on every uncollateralized debt that you can't pay. Right away.

2. Pausing and avoiding creditors as they attempt to chase you down to collect their outstanding payments. If that they have your telephone number, it is alright getting an other PDA saved for loved ones. The goal is released the account until it gets so far financially past due that they will be desperate to settle with you before charging off the account.

3. Proposing a debt settlement for as meager as 20 percent on the amount you owe. This may require some intense arrangement and standing your ground.

4. Affirming everything in writing from the creditor regarding any debt settlement and payback terms. It is prudent to not fall for a reset of the process by sending in any cash until

you have, in your grasp, the creditor's letter plotting the terms which are agreeable to you.

Once more, personal debt settlement isn't for everybody. Debt settlement will assuredly damage your credit when creditors and collection agencies continue reporting reprobate payments on your accounts.

You'll get a good deal on any charges you'd pay debt directing or combination organizations to consult for your sake. Likewise, you may have an easier time with creditors, since your creditors and collectors will realize they're dealing straightforwardly with you rather than an agent, who might be harder to work with. Creditors may go easier on you.

Finally, here's another excerpt from a Fox Business article on the subject, which I think sums the process up rather nicely:

Debt settlement experts and consumers who have the experience state your approach can make a big distinction in whether you prevail at settlement. Here are 8 tips to increase your chances:
- Get master advice. Before you dive in, counsel a tax accountant about the tax ramifications of settlement, experts state. The Internal Revenue Service includes debt discounted in a settlement as income. The exact opposite thing you have to do is transfer your credit card problems to the IRS, says Strauss.

- Plan your timeline. It's imperative to settle your debts quickly to increase your chance of progress and cut your risk of being sued, Strauss says. "12 months or less is ideal, and I'd never go past 24 months," he says. It's fundamental to investigate your accounts and assets to perceive how quickly you could concoct the money to make singular amount payments totaling 30 percent or 40 percent of your debts, he says. You ought to likewise calculate that your balance will go up around 10 percent inside the initial six months of misconduct due to interest and punishments, Strauss says.

- Know the average collection cycle. With credit card debt, an account may charge off when it's 180 days past due, Strauss says. By then, the account typically would be sent to the recuperation department of the bank, and you could begin arranging a settlement, he says. Following a month or two, it may be sent to a collection agency. After around six months, a collection agency should seriously mull over sending the debt to a collection lawyer, Strauss says.

- Find sources of money. Finding assets or different approaches to think of cash, beside simply sparing, will increase your chances of achievement, Strauss says. "Do you have an additional car you're not utilizing, or is that Harley-Davidson sitting in the garage 100 percent vital?" Strauss says. Different assets to take a gander at include collectibles, for example, baseball cards, currencies, and collectibles. Also, you can also consider renegotiating a mortgage, getting a loan from family or taking on a subsequent activity.

- Take the feeling out. "Treat debt settlement like a business," says Kenny Golde, who made an Apple store application called "Do-It-Without anyone's help Debt Settlement." Consumers will, in general, feel blame, disgrace and dread about debt they can't manage, he says. "Banks will exploit that." For them, it's only a numbers game. They're in the matter of lending money and a specific percentage of borrowers will default, Golde says.

- Set up a framework to manage calls. The average consumer settling debts has around six accounts, Strauss says. Duplicate that by a few calls every day—particularly if the collection agency resembles most and utilizes a predictive dialer (equipment or programming that increases call answer rates). "It's crazy," he says. He prescribes utilizing innovation to counterattack: Assign the collectors a quiet ring tone on your cellphone to manage calls. Charles Phelan, founder of ZipDebt.com, prescribes getting collections calls directed to another telephone—a magicJack, a subsequent cellphone or even Skype. At that point, Phelan says, tune in to the messages every day and return calls without anyone else plan.

- Explain your hardship. "You must have a hardship," says Sandee Ferman, creator of How to Settle Debts Yourself. "A hardship isn't, 'I'm not interested in paying for this big screen TV I just got.' It's you lost your employment, lost your mate, a tornado struck." It's a good plan to detail your circumstance so debt collectors can see exactly how submerged you are, says Strauss, who possesses advice on the most proficient method to converse with debt collectors on his site. The amount of evidence you have to provide will vary based on the type of debt you're attempting to settle, experts state. You won't have to provide as a lot of detail for a credit card, yet for a subsequent mortgage, you may need to provide copies of bills and tax records, Ferman says.

- Get it in writing. Regardless of whether you agree with an original creditor or a collection agency via telephone, you ought to consistently get the understanding in highly contrasting before you pay a penny, Phelan says. If that you neglect to do as such, the payment you thought would deal with your whole debt could be considered only a partial payment. "We're discussing debt collectors—They'll express anything to get you to pay," Phelan says.

The average American family has over $15,000 of credit card debt. A large number of these families are battling to make the base monthly payments, and some are utilizing plastic to cover day by day everyday costs, for example, staple goods, transportation expenses, and restorative co-pays. In spite of improving monetary conditions, increasingly more credit card clients are getting letters and telephone calls from creditors that their payments are past due.

If that you have an excess of debt and stress, right now is an ideal opportunity to stop this dangerous cycle and get the assist you with needing from a debt decrease program. This article shows you the standards of debt settlement, one of the most famous forms of debt help.

What is debt settlement?

Debt settlement- - otherwise called debt intervention, debt exchange, or credit settlement- - is a debt alleviation approach where mediators speak with creditors for your benefit to settle your debts to decreased and agreed-to amounts. Just unsecured debt-credit cards, doctor's visit expenses, and personal loans-can be arranged. You can't settle mortgages, lease, service bills, mobile phone and link charges, protection premiums, car loans, understudy loans, divorce settlement, youngster support, taxes, or criminal fines.

When you take a crack at a debt settlement program, your arrangement group opens a trust account for you. You should reserve up to half of your unsecured debt into the account over a period of 24-60 months. This money is utilized to settle your debts with creditors. Since the average debt settlement firm is revenue driven, you should likewise pay the organization a 15-25% service charge. This expense is based on the original amount of your unsecured debt or the amount arranged, depending on the debt settlement organization.

Most debt intervention organizations utilize an outsider escrow service to "stockroom" the money that they will later use to support the settlements they consult for you. The most common escrow organization is Global Client Solutions. Transferring money to your trust account is generally done through ACH around the same time every month. If that your checking account is with a bank where you additionally have a past-due loan or credit card balance, it is proposed that you utilize an alternate bank for your debt settlement program.

If you are thinking about debt settlement, here is the thing that you have to know first:

1. Debt settlement won't fathom your careless spending and savings habits. The basic way that you will accomplish enduring financial freedom is to apply the dynamic laws of financial recuperation to your regular day to day existence. These savvy money standards will assist you with establishing spending and savings habits that are based on strong bedrock. They are talked about in a separate article

entitled "The Dynamic Laws of a Successful Financial Makeover."

2. Debt settlement ought not be mistaken for bill consolidation, another type of debt decrease. Bill consolidation-otherwise called interest-rate mediation assumes your high-interest acknowledgment cards and loans and consolidates them into one, low-interest loan that you can manage. As it were, you're taking out one loan to pay off numerous others. Bill consolidation doesn't decrease the outstanding balances that you owe to creditors. It just lowers your interest rates.

3. One of the essential reasons that people pick debt discretion is to abstain from declaring financial insolvency protection. Here are five reasons why the outcomes of bankruptcy can be overpowering:

   Bankruptcy remains on your credit report for 10 years and antagonistically affects your credit score.

   Bankruptcy will tail you for the remainder of your life. For instance, many loan, credit card, and requests for employment approach If that you have ever filed for bankruptcy protection.

   Bankruptcy can't eliminate divorce settlement and youngster bolster commitments just as criminal fines.

   Aside from in limited conditions, bankruptcy can't clear out student loans.

Bankruptcy can't prevent a "verified creditor" from having a property again. According to Nolo.com: "A bankruptcy discharge eliminates debts, yet it doesn't eliminate liens. In this way, in the event that you have a verified debt, bankruptcy can eliminate the debt, however it doesn't prevent the creditor from repossesssing the property."

4. In the event that your unsecured debt is $10,000 or more, debt arbitration could spare you additional time and money than bill consolidation. Here is the reason: With debt settlement, your unsecured debt is decreased by up to half, and you won't need to pay included interest the rest of the balance. This isn't the case with bill consolidation, where is there is just a decrease in interest rates. Therefore, a debt settlement program can possess a shorter repayment term than a bill consolidation one.

5. There is no public record that you have ever settled your debts.

6. With debt arbitration, decreased balances show up as "paid in full" or "paid as settled" on your credit report.

7. Debt settlement unfavorably have a effect on your credit score.

8. Never let a debt settlement company pressure into joining their program.

9. Don't employ a company that has no interest in your particular financial needs.

10. Before you enroll in a debt arrangement program, review your financial limit carefully and make sure that you can bear the cost of the monthly payments. Don't be astounded in the event that you need to eliminate certain unimportant costs.

11. During the debt settlement , calls and letters from creditors may continue. Enrolling in a debt settlement program doesn't automatically stop "lawful collection exercises."

12. Debt arbitration can be a bet since certain creditors may decline to arrange. If this is the case, you are in the position to pay the outstanding balance on the creditor's terms.

13. As we referenced above, just unsecured debts, for example, credit cards and personal loans can be consulted to diminished amounts. You can't settle mortgages, lease, utilities, mobile phone and link bills, protection premiums, car and student loans, divorce settlement, kid support, taxes, or criminal fines.

14. You may endure tax results. For instance, if you owe $25,000 and settle for $15,000, the $10,000 contrast is viewed as taxable income. The creditor have to send you a 1099-MISC reporting a "discharge of indebtedness income."

15. A debt settlement company can't represent you in court except if it is additionally a law firm.

16. Debt arbitration can't prevent the abandonment of your home or the repossesssion of your car.

17. Regardless of admonitions from the Federal Trade Commission (FTC), some debt settlement organizations still engage in unfair strategic policies. The Federal Trade Commission prompts: "Before you enroll in a debt settlement program, get your work done. You're settling on a big decision that includes spending a great deal of your money that could be toward paying down your debt. Input the name of the company name with the word 'complaints' into a web index. Read the thing others have said about the organizations you're thinking about, including whether they are associated with a lawsuit with any state or government controllers for taking part in misleading or unfair practices."

Here are a few factors to think about while picking a debt settlement company:

1. To what extent has the company been doing business? How much business debt and consumer does the company manage every year? What number of people, families, and businesses does the company counsel yearly?

2. It is reasonable to say that you are appointed to an accomplished financial advisor to guarantee that your debt settlement program streams easily all the way?

3. Is the debt arbitration company an individual from the Online Business Bureau just as their nearby BBB? What are their ratings with the two bureaus? What kinds of complaints have been logged about their services?

4. Is the company a functioning individual from TASC, (The Association of Settlement Companies). TASC requires that the entirety of its individuals keep up a stringent arrangement of principles in working with consumers and businesses.

5. Is the debt arbitration company an individual from Dun and Bradstreet, the world's source expert for business knowledge?

Chapter 8: Loans and Your Credit Score

Loans affect your credit score more than practically some other item on your credit report. The types of loans you have, to what extent you have obtained loans, your payment history and the amounts owed on your loans has probably the biggest impact on your credit score. In the event that you can control your loans, you can support your credit score. There are a couple of tips that can get you well on your approach to easily managing your loans:

Refinance loans

In the event that you got a poor deal on a loan - particularly a significant loan, for example, a car or home loan - or if your credit rating has improved since you got your loan, you might need to consider refinancing. Refinancing implies that you take your loan to another lender so as to appreciate better terms or rates. You don't have any desire to do this time and again - it prevents you from growing long-term associations with lenders and results in inquiries on your credit report - however, in the event that you have good motivations to refinance, it can really assist you with repaying your debts. For instance, in the event that you can get progressively sensible monthly bills that you will really have the option to repay, refinancing can help prevent every one of those non-payment credit dings that originate from not having the option to pay your bills. Making your payments increasingly reasonable can save you money and can save your credit score. Temporarily, refinancing can push your credit score down, as you will obtain inquiries on your credit report as you search for another lender and as you close old accounts and open new accounts. In the long term, however, refinancing can be a good method for boosting your credit score. If that you are presently absent or postponing payments since you can't manage the cost of monthly bills, for instance, refinancing a loan or two can be a good method to refocus and can make you fix your credit score once more.

Each individual needs money. At the point when individuals need more money of their own, they have to profit loans to "account" their needs. By far most needs credit office to fulfill their financial needs, so loans and repayments are pretty much accepted as a part of "life". In this manner, individuals profit loans, and once they do, they attempt to discover available resources to "save" something out of the circumstance, since loans are related with debts, and debts show financial responsibilities and less or no savings. Individuals "need" to save money. There is one choice accessible, to the extent setting aside cash is concerned - refinance your existing loans. The essential inquiry "Is refinancing advantageous to you?", "Can you conceivable addition something through refinancing by setting aside some cash at the end of the month?", "Is refinancing advisable for you and your debt condition?". The article attempts to respond to these questions.

What is a refinance, or "refinance choice"?

Refinancing your loan intends to benefit "another" loan, which is basically an expansion of your existing loan, having an alternate arrangement of loan terms and conditions, which are progressively good regarding recovering your credit dues, and furthermore help to save some money at the month end. According to the refinance plan, your "more established" loan is "paid off" to your lender, and you start with "another" credit office having another balance, another interest rate, and new repayment options. The fundamental advantage about refinancing movement is that your interest rate, related with your new loan, is generally lower in contrast with your earlier loan rates, consequently empowering you to "save". This is maybe the most productive, and recommended method for setting aside your cash every month, in addition to your loan repayment. The refinance should be possible for some types of credit offices and loans. It is conceivable to refinance your car loan via "refinance car loan" programs or car refinance, and your existing mortgage together with a refinance mortgage programs.

Many of the auto refinance companies and banks provide offices to "refinance" existing car loans, in addition to different types of loans related to mortgage or home, and even personal loans, provided you meet the qualification criteria. The refinance is provided through mortgage refinance loans in case of mortgages, though a couple of lenders provide a similar office as home mortgage refinance. This is generally done with no additional charges, and you should simply fill out an application structure, or on the other hand, apply online. An expression of alert - most loan organizations will in general, check your credit ratings before approving your application, and your refinance request. Another issue isn't all credit foundations charge a similar interest rates. So it is recommended to check out the different refinance interest rates offered by a few lenders and banks before focusing on one particular company or lender. Doing some "explore" can assist you with profiting focused rates, and make your recovery progressively important, just as effective.

Why should I avail refinance facilities?

Considering the current economic situations and how individuals the world over are affected by the financial downturn, it is nevertheless legitimate that the average person would want to "save" as opposed to "spend". Winning and saving dollars isn't as easy as it was before. The recent past. What's more, if the individual thinks about profiting offices to "acquire" some money, or "save" some money by "doing" something, the fundamental reasoning is "the reason not?". The concept of refinancing is on a very basic level based after "saving", just as "making things easy and moderate". Refinance has evident advantages, and those advantages result into saving of money.

Possibly "a few" money, yet "unquestionably" money. Refinancing can push you to easily recover your outstanding dues, and furthermore, assist you with saving in the process. What's more, benefiting refinance is easy, you don't require uncommon qualification criteria to become "qualified" for it. Another solid inspiration is that refinance interest rates are relentlessly lessening, and according to insights, there is a progressive and prolonged diminishing in the refinance rates since some time. The fierce economic situations are equipped to deal with refinancing, and the U.S. government, just as lenders and banks are effectively supporting the concept. Another explanation, which unequivocally underpins refinance, is that the thought can be utilized for a wide range of loans, regardless of whether it be a mortgage loan, a credit card loan, a personal loan, or so far as that is concerned any legitimate and substantial loan as upheld by U.S. financial department and the law.

From where do I avail refinance facilities?

Practically all enlisted banks and financial organizations inside the U.S. bolster and provide refinance offices and programs. A couple of organizations don't bolster refinancing of any kind, yet such lenders are not many and uncommon. The point to be taken into consideration is that the refinance rates is different from bank to bank, and lender to lender. There are no set guidelines provided by the fund department, which propose the limits, or the range inside which the lenders should charge their borrowers. In addition, the FICOs make a distinction while profiting refinance options. Good scores pull in low and decreased interest rates, while poor scores welcome higher rates of interest. The good news is that few companies support refinancing exercises in any event, when the FICO is quite low, and this turns out to be a particular in addition to point for by far most of applicants who don't have not too bad credit ratings. Papers, magazines, and periodicals regularly publicize lenders and their refinance programs. One can likewise approach the credit bureaus and get a rundown of enlisted lenders. Also, the best alternative is check online for companies offering credit offices and refinance options. There are numerous such companies and organizations, in actuality, the net is proliferated with such companies. They are very easy to discover. If that you have an awful credit rating, and still want to benefit refinance offices for refinancing your car loan, companies offer the office through awful credit car refinance programs, or the terrible credit auto refinance plans, as certain experts prefer to call it. A similar remain constant for mortgage refinance, in which case it is awful credit mortgage refinance programs, and terrible credit home mortgage refinance plans individually.

When shopping to lower your loan costs, you need to realize the most reduced mortgage refinance rates. This will give you the best bank for your well deserved bucks, particularly in an unsure economy. Don't settle for only asking your nearby mortgage lenders, you may really locate a superior deal online.

Amusing thing is about the least mortgage refinance rates, you can shop and look at, however in the event that you have a mortgage lender or company you prefer, you can return to them on rates after you have found the best rate and have them coordinate it. Let's be honest, in the event that you were in the mortgage refinance business, you need to take full advantage of the consumer, however, faced with losing a loan, you will reexamine If that you are faced with a smart borrower.

Remember that finding the most minimal mortgage refinance rates isn't generally in the interest rates alone. Mortgage interest rates are just part of the condition. You have to analyze markdown focuses also interest rates. If that a mortgage lender has the most minimal refinance rates however higher markdown focuses, you might need to set that mortgage lender against the following closest lender and play one against the other for the most flawlessly awesome deal.

Whenever you are thinking about refinancing your existing mortgage, the time left on the existing loan is urgent to an accurate examination in getting the best deal along with the most reduced mortgage refinance rates. If that you have over a large portion of your existing mortgage paid down, you might need to take a gander at a shorter loan payback or perhaps simply getting serious about a payment in any event once every year to give a superior payoff time line than just searching for the most reduced mortgage refinance rates.

Rarely will a mortgage lender give all of you the realities that will profit you as a borrower, so make sure you have quite a few questions recorded, before reaching a mortgage lender. Make certain to get some information about markdown focuses, loan start expenses, garbage charges, and some other exceptional charges doled out from each mortgage lender. They are ready to go to make the most from you, so a smart borrower will do his/her homework first.

Most mortgage refinance deals take into consideration every single forthright cost to be folded into the new mortgage, so here is a slippery method to get more money folded into the new mortgage with the goal that more interest can be collected over the life of the loan. In the event that you can bear to pay out of pocket for the refinance costs, you'll save much more money in the deal. The most reduced mortgage refinance rates will generally be cited from mid-week and around the week's end. Monday is a terrible day to get mortgage loan rate cites. Lenders will alter their mortgage rates descending as a rule as the week progresses and the process rehashes the next week.

Junk expenses are simply the best spot to save some big money. Junk charges are add-on costs for working with a particular lender. Every lender attempts their best to get more cash from you when you aren't paying consideration. Like it was said before, the lender is tied in with getting more cash for the company as opposed to helping you. Demand a rundown of junk charges. They'll recognize what you are discussing and should confess all with them If that they plan on working with you.

You might not be right in the event that you think getting a poor credit refinance is outlandish. There are ways that you can verify an awful credit refinance even in the present tight credit showcase.

There are options or strategies that are basic and effective that will support a great many people. It positively makes sense that the interest for poor credit refinance in expanding in view of the problems with the economy. What's more, it isn't simply United States economy yet, in addition, the financial emergency confronting most nations on the planet.

In the event that you happen to have good credit, at that point you will have no problems finding approaches to refinance your home loan, it will be fast and easy.

Yet, for those with terrible credit, they will have a progressively troublesome time attempting to get their home refinanced, however it conceivable to get a poor credit refinance. It will require some information and furthermore some work to get a refinancing loan for your home in the event that you have terrible credit scores.

Here are some basic and effective ways to obtain a poor credit refinance.

Improve Your Credit Scores

If you have good credit scores you will have more chances to refinance and furthermore, you will show signs of improvement interest rate.

In this way, if your credit scores are not exactly consummate it makes sense to improve them. It is never past the stage where it is possible to make the strides that are important to improve your credit record. What can you do to improve your credit scores?

In the first place, you have to repay the entirety of your current debts and bills. You could likewise verified some extremely small loans and afterward, pay them off fast just to show to lenders that you pay your bills on time.

By taking out small loans and repaying them you will have the option to get a poor credit home loan refinance all the more quickly.

Investigate Your Credit Records

If you haven't took a gander at your credit history as of late, at that point you should. There might be errors or loans on your credit record that are not yours or loans that have been paid off yet not removed from your credit record. This is something that should effortlessly be possible and it won't require some investment. It could likewise incredibly increase your credit score.

Breaking down your credit history will give you some information about how the process functions and that it is so important to pay your bills on time.

Finding Poor Credit Refinance Lenders

There are a great deal of lenders that will provide terrible credit home loans; however, you do need to find a respectable one. It is ideal to adhere to the top lenders. You have to do your exploration. You have to find a solid poor credit refinance lender and you can do this by correlation shopping. Search the Internet and look at the lenders and quest for reviews on the lenders.

You are not the only one. An ongoing report expresses that 25% of all Americans have a credit score under 599. In the present market, you will require a credit score of 620 and higher to get a home loan. However, in the event that you are eager to do a tad of work you will be able to get a poor credit refinance loan!

Search for loans that are offered for terrible credit risks

If your credit score is awful however you need a loan, consider services that oblige people with poor credit scores. These companies realize that a few creditors with poor credit scores will, in any case, make their payments on time as are happy to speak with debtors different companies would dismiss without a second thought. You may need to deal with higher interest rates, yet picking an awful credit lender can go a long method to guaranteeing that your credit score won't disqualify you for a loan. Over the long haul, you can generally refinance your loan to exploit a superior rate once your credit score improves.

Continuously realize your credit score before speaking to lenders

Numerous people accept that having a magnificent credit score is sufficient while applying for a loan. It isn't. A few lenders are not horrendously trustworthy about offering you the best rate - particularly in the event that they can pick up by having you pay higher interest. A few lenders will attempt to reveal to you that your credit score is lower than it is and that precludes you from a superior rate. Some may depend on your ignorance (or what they think about your ignorance) about your credit score to quote you a more regrettable rate. Never let a lender do this. Continuously look into your credit score before shopping for a significant loan, and If that you are quoted a rate you believe is unfair, talk and inform the credit officer that a credit score of 650 (or whatever the score is) appears to demonstrate a superior loan. Bring out and show the lender your printed copy of your credit score. In the event that the lender attempts to reveal to you that lenders get more accurate credit scores than customers who look into their own credit scores or attempts to disclose to you that your credit score has changed, leave. There are numerous respectable lenders out there. Find one of them as opposed to depending on a lender who will attempt to mislead make a profit.

Consider speaking to lenders face-to-face if you have a terrible credit score

In the event that you apply for a loan via phone or online, your credit score will tally the most, in light of the fact that that is all the lender will probably take a gander at before hitting you up with a quote. In the event that you have terrible credit yet at the same time require a loan, talking with a lender face to face is your most logical option on the grounds that a genuine gathering enables a lender to get an impression of you, and enables you to clarify the problems you have had before and the things you are doing now to make yourself a superior credit risk. At the point when you meet worth a lender in person, you drive them to quit taking a gander at you as a credit score number and make them take a gander at you as a whole person. This can be a tremendous advantage for you (particularly in the event that you are personable) and can assist you with getting the loan your credit score doesn't totally qualify you for.

How to Fix Your Credit Score